Social Issues
in Literature

Racism in
Harper Lee's
To Kill a Mockingbird

Other Books in the Social Issues in Literature Series:

Social Issues
in Literature

Racism in
Harper Lee's
To Kill a Mockingbird

Candice Mancini, Book Editor

GREENHAVEN PRESS
A part of Gale, Cengage Learning

GALE
CENGAGE Learning™

Detroit • New York • San Francisco • New Haven, Conn • Waterville, Maine • London

Christine Nasso, *Publisher*
Elizabeth Des Chenes, *Managing Editor*

© 2008 Greenhaven Press, a part of Gale, Cengage Learning.

For more information, contact:
Greenhaven Press
27500 Drake Rd.
Farmington Hills, MI 48331-3535
Or you can visit our Internet site at gale.cengage.com

Articles in Greenhaven Press anthologies are often edited for length to meet page require-ments. In addition, original titles of these works are changed to clearly present the main thesis and to explicitly indicate the author's opinion. Every effort is made to ensure that Greenhaven Press accurately reflects the original intent of the authors. Every effort has been made to trace the owners of copyrighted material.

Cover photograph reproduced by permission of John Vacha/FPG/Getty Images.

LIBRARY OF CONGRESS CATALOGING-IN-PUBLICATION DATA

Racism in Harper Lee's To Kill a Mockingbird / Candice Mancini, book editor.
    p. cm. -- (Social issues in literature)
  Includes bibliographical references and index.
  ISBN-13: 978-0-7377-3900-8 (hardcover)
  ISBN-10: 0-7377-3900-2 (hardcover)
  ISBN-13: 978-0-7377-3904-6 (pbk.)
  ISBN-10: 0-7377-3904-5 (pbk.)
  1. Lee, Harper. To kill a mockingbird. 2. Racism in literature. 3. Justice in literature.
I. Mancini, Candice.
  PS3562.E353T645 2008
  813'.54--dc22
                                              2007040011

Printed in the United States of America
2 3 4 5 6 7 12 11 10 09 08

Contents

Chapter 1: Background on Harper Lee

Chapter 2: *To Kill a Mockingbird* and Racism

Chapter 3: Contemporary Perspectives on Racism

Introduction

Setting—a time and place, a family, and a community—determines so much in a life: day-to-day routine, principles, integrity, and passions. Whether setting is embraced, opposed, or both, its impact is undeniable. Harper Lee was born in 1926 in Monroeville, Alabama, the daughter of a southern lawyer. If nothing were known of her beyond this, if there were no access to individual pieces that have made up her life—if there were no *To Kill a Mockingbird*—how would her setting be envisioned? It's possible the vision would be shaped, at least in part, by a southern romanticism endorsed by so many books, films, and by oral history. In this romanticized image, the Alabama of Lee's childhood is made up of tree-lined small towns, wraparound porches, and agriculture stretched over miles of green landscape. The air is hot and humid; it is a place where flowers and insects thrive.

Studies of history and sociology have revealed the complicated layers within this setting, however. Harper Lee was born just eight years after the end of World War I, a battle that claimed over 6,000 Alabamian lives. In the 1930s the entire nation was marked by the Great Depression; in Alabama, an agricultural depression had already begun the previous decade. Beyond the wraparound porches were countless shanty towns filled with sheet-metal shacks, residences of southern poor, both black and white.

Even amongst the poor, there were social divisions: at the bottom of the social rung, even below the poorest whites, were those who only two generations before would have been slaves. In *To Kill a Mockingbird*, this poor white bigotry was personified through Bob Ewell. But this situation, too, had layers: the blacks gave poor whites a feeling of superiority and a sense of credibility. Without the black residents, poor whites

would have been clear down at the bottom of the rung with nowhere to look beyond themselves but up.

The racism that existed in 1930s Alabama, though, was facilitated by poor and well-to-do alike; it was a racism justified by segregation, a racism that was distinct, unambiguous, and as much the way of life as was farming, or finding shade on a hot August afternoon. The setting was, in the words of Glenn Fieldman in *Politics, Society, and the Klan in Alabama*, the most unenlightened "piece of turf in America" with "the worst record of any state in the country on human and civil liberties."

Harper Lee was witness, from a young age, to these atrocities of human and civil liberties. She was five years old when the Scottsboro Trials—in which nine black men were accused of raping two white women—began in Scottsboro, Alabama. When she was eight, a black man named Walter Lett was accused of raping a white woman; the case, which ended in a death sentence for Lett, was tried in Lee's Monroeville County. White citizens wrote anonymously to Alabama's governor claiming Lett had been falsely accused, but his death sentence was merely exchanged for life in prison. Because it was so close to home and because she was a bit older, perhaps it was this case, more than Scottsboro, that shaped Tom Robinson's trial in *To Kill a Mockingbird*.

Although set in the 1930s, it can be argued that events of later years too shaped Lee's novel. In 1954, the U.S. Supreme Court's *Brown vs. Board of Education* decision overturned segregation in schools. Whereas segregation advocates maintained fairness in "separate but equal" schools, *Brown* insisted that separate was not, in fact, equal, and that racial segregation violated the Constitution's 14th Amendment. The overturning of segregation increased the violence shown toward blacks, as could be witnessed in the 1955 murder of Emmett Till, a fourteen-year-old African American boy who died because he whistled at a white woman in Mississippi. Once acquitted,

Till's white murderers bragged to the media about what they had done. It's easy to imagine the story having personal impact on Harper Lee, who was, around that time, writing her novel.

Even so, with *To Kill a Mockingbird*, Lee did not overtly attack southern human rights violations. She did not tell of Klansmen in white gowns terrorizing blacks; she portrayed no actual lynching (although in a well-known scene, Scout prevents a possible lynching while her father stands guard outside Tom Robinson's jail cell). Nor did Lee condemn all of white Alabama society as evil. What she did was provide evidence that racism, itself, was evil. But her way of doing so has been the source of criticism from all directions. Several have found the novel inadequate in its representation of the black perspective and some have thought Lee not ruthless enough in her condemnation of racism. In contrast, others have complained that her depiction of southern white society was too harsh.

Regardless of how her technique is viewed, her portrayal of a black man falsely accused of raping a white woman is an honest one. With *To Kill a Mockingbird*, Harper Lee portrayed an understanding of what was perhaps Atticus Finch's most valuable lesson: "You never really understand a person until you consider things from his point of view—until you climb into his skin and walk around in it." Through her ability to do so, Harper Lee offered to readers a snapshot of a setting—a time and place, a family, and a community—that she both embraced and opposed.

The articles that follow explore racism as portrayed by Lee in *To Kill a Mockingbird* and examine the ongoing issue of racism today.

Chronology

1926

Nelle Harper Lee is born on April 28, in Monroeville, Alabama, to Amasa Coleman (A.C.) Lee and Frances Finch Lee.

1944–1945

Lee attends Huntingdon College.

1945–1949

Lee studies law at the University of Alabama.

1949

Six months short of a law degree, Lee moves to New York City, taking a job as a reservations clerk with an airline. (She soon quits to work full-time on her writing.)

1957

Lee submits her manuscript (which would become *To Kill a Mockingbird*) to J.B. Lippincott Company, but it needs revision. She works on it for two and a half more years.

1959

Lee accompanies Truman Capote to Holcombe, Kansas, to work as his research assistant for his book *In Cold Blood*.

1960

To Kill a Mockingbird is published by Lippincott.

1961

Lee is awarded the Pulitzer Prize, the Alabama Library Association award, and the Brotherhood Award of National Conference of Christians and Jews for *To Kill a Mockingbird*.

1961

Lee publishes articles in *Vogue* and *McCalls*.

1962

To Kill a Mockingbird wins *Bestsellers'* Paperback of the Year Award. That year, it is also made into a film starring Gregory Peck, who wins the Academy Award for Best Actor.

1966

Lee is appointed by President Lyndon Johnson to the National Council of Arts.

1983

Lee presents an essay at the Alabama History and Heritage Festival.

1987

To Kill a Mockingbird is adapted as a stage play in London.

2002

Lee wins the Alabama Humanities Award for *To Kill a Mockingbird*.

Social Issues
in Literature

Background on
Harper Lee

The Life of Harper Lee

Dorothy Jewell Altman

Dorothy Jewell Altman is an assistant professor at Bergen Community College.

Although she published only one novel, with To Kill a Mockingbird *Harper Lee made a significant contribution to literary history. While critics have suggested that her book was autobiographical, Lee has stressed otherwise. Still, Lee has conceded that writers should write what they know. As such, through her experience as a southern daughter of a lawyer, Lee bestowed readers with a snapshot of a 1930s American southern town. Through the voice of its child narrator, Jean Louise "Scout" Finch, a melodic story—reverberating with opposing themes of ignorance-knowledge; cowardice-heroism; guilt-innocence; and prejudice (persecution)-tolerance—came to life. Lee's mastery of symbolism, seen in the ever-present allusion to the mockingbird, is one of the features in* To Kill a Mockingbird *most commonly praised.*

Harper Lee's reputation as an author rests on her only novel, *To Kill a Mockingbird* (1960). An enormous popular success, the book was selected for distribution by the Literary Guild and the Book-of-the-Month Club and was published in a shortened version as a *Reader's Digest* condensed book. It was also made into an Academy Award–winning film in 1962. Moreover, the novel was critically acclaimed, winning among other awards the Pulitzer Prize for fiction (1961), the Brotherhood Award of the National Conference of Christians and Jews (1961), and the *Bestsellers* magazine's Paperback of the Year Award (1962).

Dorothy Jewell Altman, from *Dictionary of Literary Biography, Volume 6: American Novelists Since World War II*, Second Series, A Bruccoli Clark Layman Book. Farmington Hills, MI: The Gale Group, 1980. Edited by James E. Kobler, Jr. Reproduced by permission.

Writers Should Write What They Know

Although Lee stresses that *To Kill a Mockingbird* is not auto-biographical, she allows that a writer "should write about what he knows and write truthfully." The time period and setting of the novel obviously originate in the author's experience as the youngest of three children born to lawyer Amasa Coleman Lee (related to Robert E. Lee) and Frances Finch Lee. The family lived in the sleepy little town of Monroeville, Alabama. After graduating from Monroevile's public schools, Lee spent a year (1944–1945) at Huntingdon College in Montgomery, Alabama, and then attended the University of Alabama for four years (1945–1949), including a year as an exchange student at Oxford University. She left the University of Alabama in 1950, six months short of a law degree, to pursue a writing career in New York City.

Lee's Background

Harper Lee became interested in writing at the age of seven. While she was a student at the University of Alabama, her satires, editorial columns, and reviews appeared in campus publications.

Living in New York in the early 1950s and supporting herself by working as an airline reservations clerk, she approached a literary agent with the manuscripts of two essays and three short stories. The agent encouraged her to expand one of the stories into a novel which later became *To Kill a Mockingbird*.

With the financial help of friends, she gave up her job and moved into a cold-water flat where she devoted herself to her writing. Although her father became ill and she was forced to divide her time between New York and Monroeville, she continued to work on her novel. She submitted a manuscript to Lippincott in 1957. While editors criticized the book's structure, suggesting it seemed to be a series of short stories strong together, they recognized the novel's promise and encouraged

Lee to rewrite it. With the help of her editor, Tay Hohoff, Lee reworked the material, and *To Kill a Mockingbird* was finally published in July 1960.

Key Interests in the Novel

To Kill a Mockingbird is narrated by Jean Louise "Scout" Finch, a six-year-old girl who lives with her ten-year-old brother Jem and her lawyer father Atticus in the small Alabama town of Maycomb during the 1930s. During the three years covered by the novel, Scout and Jem gain an increased understanding of the adult world. A key incident in their maturing is the legal defense by their father of Tom Robinson, a black man falsely accused of raping a white girl named Mayella Ewell, daughter of the nefarious Bob Ewell. In the months preceding the trial, Scout and Jem suffer the taunts of classmates and neighbors who object to Atticus's "lawing for niggers." As the trial nears, the situation intensifies, and a threatened lynching of Robinson is narrowly averted by the innocent intervention of Jem and Scout. In a climactic scene, the jury finds Robinson guilty even though Atticus has clearly proven him innocent. Maycomb's racial prejudice is so engrained that Atticus cannot influence the verdict of people reared to believe "that *all* Negroes lie, that *all* Negroes are basically immoral beings, that *all* Negro men are not to be trusted around . . . [white] women."

Another major interest in the novel is the unraveling of the mystery surrounding the neighborhood recluse Arthur "Boo" Radley, who has remained secluded in the Radley house since he was arrested many years before for some teenage pranks and then released in his father's custody. Initially a victim of his father's uncompromising religion and family pride, Boo gradually becomes a victim of community prejudice, feared by adults and children alike. When Jem and Scout befriend Dill, a little boy who is spending summers in Maycomb with his aunt, the three devote themselves to Dill's idea of making Boo come out. At first the children imagine that the

Harper Lee and her father A.C. Lee relax at the Lee home in Monroeville, Alabama during a 1961 visit by Ms. Lee to her home town. Mr. Lee is thought to have been the inspiration for To Kill a Mockingbird's *Atticus Finch.* Donald Uhrbrock/Time & Life Pictures/Getty Images.

recluse dines on raw squirrels and roams the neighborhood by night. But finally they learn that Boo is truly a friend who has

done a number of kind deeds for them. He hides gifts for the children in a hollow tree. He secretly mends Jem's torn pants, which were badly snagged on the Radleys' fence and abandoned there by the boy during an attempt to spy on Boo. Boo leaves them on the fence for Jem to retrieve. One cold winter night, while Scout stands shivering near the Radleys' steps as she watches a neighbor's house burn, Boo, unseen, covers her with a blanket. Finally, it is Boo who rescues Scout and Jem from the murderous attack of drunken, vengeful Bob Ewell.

To Kill a Mockingbird's Opposing Themes and Symbols

To Kill a Mockingbird contains a number of complex and opposing themes in a deceptively simple narrative—ignorance-knowledge, cowardice-heroism, guilt-innocence, and prejudice (persecution)-tolerance. The ignorance-knowledge theme is developed through characterization and action. Lee believes that children are born with an instinct for truth and justice. Their education, which is the result of observing the behavior of the adults around them, can nurture or destroy their intrinsic goodness. Fortunately, the Finch children have Atticus to provide the true education that the Maycomb school fails to provide. The structuring of the action around the Boo Radley mystery and Robinson's trial is well suited to the gradual revelation of truth and further develops the ignorance-knowledge theme.

The character most central to the development of the cowardice-heroism theme is Atticus Finch; in counterpoint to Atticus's courage is the bullying cowardice of Bob Ewell. In part one of the novel, the children begin to think of their father as a hero when they see him shoot a rabid dog and learn for the first time that he was once "the deadest shot in Maycomb County." Atticus reforms the children's definition of courage when he has Jem read to Mrs. Dubose, a former drug addict, after school. The day after she dies, he tells Jem about

her victory over morphine: "I wanted you to see what real courage is, instead of getting the idea that courage is a man with a gun in his hand. It's when you're licked before you begin but you begin anyway and you see it through no matter what." In part two of the novel, Atticus fulfills this definition of courage in defending Tom Robinson.

The themes of guilt-innocence and prejudice (persecution)-tolerance are closely related in the novel. The characters who are innocent—Tom Robinson and Boo Radley—are judged guilty by a prejudiced society. Tom is killed trying to escape from prison but the novel expresses hope that prejudice will be overcome. Jem sheds tears at the end of the trial and vows to combat racial injustice. However, the climax of the trial is melodramatic, and the narrative flounders when characters mouth pious speeches against prejudice.

Lee's use of symbol is masterful. The mockingbird closely associated with Boo Radley and Tom Robinson represents joy and innocence. Both Atticus and Miss Maudie, an optimistic neighbor, tell the children that it is a sin to kill a mockingbird. Lee's use of the symbolic mockingbird has been compared to [poet Walt] Whitman's in "Out of the Cradle Endlessly Rocking." When Maycomb has a light snowfall for the first time in years, Jem builds a snowman underlaid with mud to give it sufficient substance. The snowman melts when Miss Maudie's house burns. Thus, in a day the snowman's color goes from black to white and from white to black, proving how superficial skin color is.

Critical Feedback of *To Kill a Mockingbird*

When *To Kill a Mockingbird* appeared in 1960, its critical reception was mixed. R. W. Henderson called it "a compassionate, deeply moving novel, and a most persuasive plea for racial justice"; others praised Lee's "insight into Southern mores" and her "wit, grace, and skill." Negative comments were made about the novel's sermonizing and its melodramatic climax.

Some critics found fault with the point of view. In *Atlantic* Phoebe Adams found the story "frankly and completely impossible, being told in the first person by a six-year-old girl, with the prose style of a well-educated adult." Granville Hicks noted in *Saturday Review* that "Miss Lee's problem has been to tell the story she wants to tell and yet to stay within the consciousness of a child, and she hasn't consistently solved it."

Scholars writing articles about the novel in the 1970s praise its technical excellence and recognize its place in literary tradition. R. A. Dave notes that in creating the small world of Maycomb, Lee has made "an epic canvas against which is enacted a movingly human drama of the jostling worlds—of children and adults, of innocence and experience, of kindness and cruelty, of love and hatred, of humor and pathos, and above all of appearance and reality—all taking the reader to the root of human behavior."

Fred Erisman in "The Romantic Regionalism of Harper Lee" [published in *Alabama Review*] notes Lee's awareness of traditional Southern romanticism and its pervasive influence on the South, but suggests that she sees the beginning of a new type of romanticism, "the more reasonable, pragmatic, and native romanticism of a Ralph Waldo Emerson [an American writer and transcendentalist]."

With the novel's dramatic success, articles and interviews about Lee appeared in leading periodicals. The author of a 1961 *Newsweek* interview suggests that Lee "strongly calls to mind the impish tomboy who narrates her novel. There is a faint touch of gray in her Italian boy haircut and a heavy touch of Alabama in her accent."

Lee's Contribution of Self and Literature

In interviews Lee's quick wit served to protect her privacy. She describes herself as a Whig ("I believe in Catholic emancipation and repeal of the Corn Laws") and quotes as her favorite fan letter one which accuses her of playing down the serious problem of the rape of white women ("Why is it that you young Jewish authors seek to whitewash the situation?"); she fabricated a clever response signed "Harper Levy."

She did, however, speak seriously in interviews about her reading tastes and her work habits. She numbered among her favorite authors Charles Lamb [an English essayist], Robert Louis Stevenson ("the old gentleman"), Jane Austen ("writing, cameo-like, in that little corner of the world of hers and making it universal"), and Thomas Love Peacock [an English satirist], as well as various religious memorialists of the nineteenth century. Describing herself as a "journeyman writer," she noted that "writing is the hardest thing in the world, . . . but writing is the only thing that has made me completely happy." In 1961 she was in Monroeville working on her second novel, which was also to have a Southern setting. She said that she began working about noon, after sleeping late, and worked until early evening. Because her method involved extensive revision, she completed only a page or two each day.

The reading public and the critics have been eagerly awaiting more of Lee's writing. In the early 1960s, several short pieces about personal experiences and an article discussing different types of love, "Love—in Other Words," appeared in popular magazines; none of her work has been published since. . . . Although she travels extensively, Monroeville, where her sister Alice Lee practices law, remains home. Whether or not Harper Lee adds to her body of published work, her contribution to American literature is an important one. *To Kill a Mockingbird*, a regional novel with a universal message, combines popular appeal with literary excellence, assuring Harper Lee's place in American letters.

To Kill a Mockingbird's Racism Stems from History

Charles Shields

Charles Shields is a former English teacher and a prolific writer of young-adult nonfiction.

Even if not fully autobiographical, To Kill a Mockingbird *was based on Nelle Harper Lee's childhood. For one, the attorney father of the novel, Atticus Finch, was modeled after Lee's attorney father, A. C. Lee. Another striking similarity between life and book rests on the story's narrator, Jean Louise "Scout" Finch. The experiences of Scout and her family—including the story of the rabid dog and the attempt to lure Boo Radley, the town recluse, out of his house—mirrored childhood experiences of Harper Lee. Lee's childhood friend, Truman Capote (who was purported to be the inspiration for the character of Dill), confirmed that most of the characters in* To Kill a Mockingbird *were based on real-life people from Lee's childhood.*

The potential of Walter Lett's [a black man arrested for raping a poor white woman near Monroeville, where Lee grew up] trial to inspire sympathy, and its power to cast light on a racist judicial system in a small, manageable setting, made it [a good] choice in Nelle [Harper Lee]'s mind for her novel's foundation. . . . She knew the details of the Lett case well, as do many older people who still live in Monroeville. And in her mind's eye, too, she could see the hero, the attorney in charge of a fictionalized version of Lett's defense, fitting inside the Monroe County Courthouse with ease, because she had seen him there many times—he was her own father, A. C. Lee.

In fact, in November 1919, Mr. Lee had defended two Negroes accused of murder. In those days, an inexperienced twenty-nine-year-old attorney with only four years of practice under his belt, he was appointed by the court to argue his first criminal case. He did his utmost, but lost, as he was destined to do, given the times. Both his clients were hanged and afterward mutilated, with pieces of their bloody scalps mailed in a gruesome Christmas package to their victim's son in Irvington, New York, as proof that "justice" had been done. Using the remedial power of fiction, however, Nelle had a free hand to retell this macabre episode in her father's life, which he always referred to in vague terms, no doubt because of the pain it caused him. (He never accepted another criminal case.) This time, under his daughter's sensitive hand, A. C. Lee, in the character of Atticus Finch, could be made to argue in defense of Walter Lett, and his virtues as a humane, fair-minded man would be honored.

Worth pointing out, however, is that Mr. Lee himself only gradually rose to the moral standards of Atticus. Though more enlightened than most, A. C. was no saint, no prophet crying in the wilderness with regard to racial matters. In many ways, he was typical of his generation, especially about issues surrounding integration. Like most of his generation, he believed that the current social order, segregation, was natural and created harmony between the races. It was a point not even worth discussing that blacks and whites were different. As the Bible said, "In my Father's house are many mansions." That divine structure's great roof covered all humanity. Hence, blacks deserved consideration and charity as fellow creatures of God and the law should protect them. But they were not the same as white people, and for that simple reason—to continue the biblical metaphor—they did not need to be in the same room with whites. . . .

A. C. Lee changed his views about race relations during the . . . 1950s. And Nelle watched as her father, formerly a conservative on matters of race and social progress, became an advocate for the rights of Negroes. Part of the reason for his change of mind was the influence of events that no thoughtful American in the 1950s could ignore. In 1954, two white men murdered Emmett Till, a fourteen-year-old Negro visiting Alabama from his home in Chicago, for whistling at a white woman. The killers were acquitted, and then bragged about their crime to the media. Two years later, Autherine Lucy, a black student, attempted to enroll at Nelle's alma mater, the University of Alabama, but violence on the campus for three days forced her to flee. Despite a court order to re-admit her, the Board of Trustees barred her from campus. Former Alabama state senator J. M. Bonner, whom A. C. Lee probably knew from his own career in the statehouse, wrote to the *Tuscaloosa News*, "I call now on every Southern White man to join in this fight. I proudly take my stand with those students who resisted, and who will continue to resist the ad-mission of a negress named Lucy."

A contest of warring principles was gearing up in the South, and a civic-minded man like A. C. Lee could not fail to recognize it happening in his own backyard. In 1959, the Ku Klux Klan forced the cancellation of the annual Monroeville Christmas parade by threatening to kill any members of the all-Negro Union High School band who participated. The morning after the parade was cancelled, A. C. walked into the store owned by A. B. Blass, noting that the store's facade had been vandalized with racist graffiti. As president of Kiwanis, Blass had made the decision to call off the parade for safety's sake. "Mr. Lee came down to our store from his office and knowing what we had done put his hand on my shoulder," said Blass, "looked me in the eye and said, 'Son, you did the right thing.'"

By the time *To Kill a Mockingbird* was published, A. C. counted himself an activist in defending the civil rights of Ne-groes. In 1962, while a reporter was interviewing Nelle at her home in Monroeville, Alice [her sister] and A. C. stopped by on their way to the offices of Bugg, Barnett & Lee. The eighty-one-year-old A. C. interrupted to speak earnestly about the importance of reapportioning voting districts to provide fairer representation for Negro voters. "It's got to be done," he said.

Though this was not a reversal in so many words of his stand a decade earlier on the importance of keeping the church out of secular affairs, it was clear that racial equity had become a matter of conscience for A. C.; and so a religious man, such as he was, had to confront his conviction about justice and humanity. . . .

With the core components of her novel in place, Nelle set to work revising *Atticus* [the original name of the manuscript that became *To Kill a Mockingbird*] in the winter of 1957. As any successful novelist must do, she needed to create a fictional reality, a unique landscape for her reader to enter. So the setting of *To Kill a Mockingbird* is Maycomb, Alabama, a town similar to Monroeville. The time is the Depression, and Maycomb County is so poor that the energy of life itself seems to be on hold. "People moved slowly then," Lee writes. "They ambled across the square, shuffled in and out of stores around it, took their time about everything. A day was twenty-four hours long but seemed longer. There was no hurry, for there was nowhere to go, nothing to buy and no money to buy it with, nothing to see outside the boundaries of Maycomb County."

Lee's time frame is a three-year period in Maycomb between the summer of 1932 and Halloween night 1935. [Truman] Capote [author and childhood friend of Lee] later said that the first two-thirds of the book, the portion about Scout, Dill, and Jem (Nelle, Truman, and Nelle's brother, Edwin, probably) trying to coax Boo Radley out of his house, "are quite literal and true." Supporting this is the way actual incidents reported by the *Monroe Journal* during those years became part of the fabric of the story. For instance, in February 1933, when Nelle was six years old, a Mr. Dees fired a shotgun at somebody prowling in his collard patch, which parallels Nathan Radley firing a load of buckshot in Jem Finch's direction while he was retrieving his pants from the Radley's backyard. In May 1934, a rabid dog bit two adults and two children, prefiguring the scene in the novel of Atticus shooting a mad dog.

To populate the streets of Maycomb, Lee thought back on the inhabitants of Monroeville in the early 1930s: its officials, merchants, churchgoers, and even the local ne'er-do-wells. After the novel was published, some Monroeville folks believed they recognized themselves and neighbors. Capote made no bones about telling friends, "Most of the people in Nelle's book are drawn from life."

An interesting twist about the novel is that there are two first-person narrative voices: the first is Jean Louise Finch, nicknamed "Scout." She talks, thinks, and acts like a six- to nine-year-old girl—albeit a very bright one—who perceives her world and the people in it as only an insatiably curious (and garrulous) child could. The second narrator is Scout, too, now an adult known as Jean Louise Finch, looking back on events with the benefit of hindsight. Sometimes the voices will alternate. For example, the adult Jean will set the stage:

> When I was almost six and Jem was nearly ten, our summertime boundaries (within calling distance of Calpurnia) were Mrs. Henry Lafayette Dubose's house two doors to the north of us, and the Radley Place three doors to the south. We were never tempted to break them. The Radley Place was inhabited by an entity the mere description of whom was enough to make us behave for days on end; Mrs. Dubose was plain hell.

> That was the summer Dill came to us.

Harper Lee stops in at the local courthouse while visiting her home town of Monroeville, Alabama. Donald Uhrbrock/Time & Life Pictures/Getty Images.

Then six-year-old Scout describes the actual moment Dill appeared, and drama replaces exposition. In a cinematic sense, the narration provided by the adult Jean Louise is like a voice-over.

A few critics later found fault with this technique. Phoebe Adams in the *Atlantic* dismissed the story as "frankly and completely impossible, being told in the first person by a six-year-old girl with the prose style of a well-educated adult." Granville Hicks wrote in the *Saturday Review* that "Lee's problem has been to tell the story she wants to tell and yet to stay within the consciousness of a child, and she hasn't consistently solved it." W. J. Stuckey, in *The Pulitzer Prize Novels: A Critical Backward Look*, attributed Lee's "rhetorical trick" to a failure to solve "the technical problems raised by her story and whenever she gets into difficulties with one point of view, she switches to the other."

It might be that Lee floundered when she was trying to settle on a point of view. She rewrote the novel three times:

the original draft was in the third person, then she changed to the first person and later rewrote the final draft, which blended the two narrators, Janus-like, looking forward and back at the same time [Janus is a god from Roman mythology depicted with two faces]. She later called this a "hopeless period" of writing the novel over and over.

Aside from what Nelle's intention might have been, the effort involved was more frustrating than she imagined it would be. The writing went at a glacial pace. A perfectionist, Nelle was more of a "rewriter" than a writer, she admitted later. She "spent her days and nights in the most intense efforts to set down what she wanted to say in the way which would best say it to the reader," said [her editor, Theresa von (Tay)] Hohoff. While working out of her apartment in New York, she lived on pennies, according to friends, still typing at the makeshift desk on York Avenue she had hammered together years earlier. No one "inquired too closely into what she ate," although now and then, Sue Philipp from Monroeville, . . . who was living in New York at the time, invited Nelle over for a square meal and the chance to talk about how things were going on the book. Then, for months at a time, Nelle returned to Monroeville.

She did so reluctantly, because it was no treat returning home to a humdrum existence for long stretches, sometimes four to six months. She was bored to tears. Having lived a cosmopolitan life, being without bookstores, museums, better restaurants, and so on. Why did she do it, and continue to do it, year after year?

Conceivably, Alice could argue that she had always been the one to step into the breach for the family—joining the law firm, supervising her mother's care, and now caring for A. C. For thirty years, Alice had "kept the home fires burning," as she liked to say, while her other siblings had moved away or married. Now, Nelle was a bohemian in New York and jobless while she lived on her advance for the book. She had no responsibilities other than to herself, while Alice had put her life on hold. It didn't seem fair, to put it simply. Moreover, Nelle could write in Monroeville or New York; which, in fact, she did when she took the train to Monroeville. She found a room at the country club and wrote without interruption.

Regardless, it was a return under duress to the life she had wanted to leave behind. Sometimes, just to get away, she would go into the country to Truman's aunt Mary Ida Carter's house, along with her favorite brand of scotch or gin, and just hang out there for long afternoons, reading and sipping. "Mr. Lee and Alice didn't want to see it or know about it," said Mary Ida's sister, Marie Faulk Rudisill. It was Nelle's quiet way of rebelling.

When she returned to New York after a long hiatus down South, she and Hohoff met to discuss the book's progress. Hohoff remembered, "we talked it out, sometimes for hours. And sometimes she came around to my way of thinking, sometimes I to hers, sometimes the discussion would open up an entirely new line of country." (She concurred with Nelle about changing the title to *To Kill a Mockingbird* from *Atticus*, and about Nelle calling herself Harper Lee. Nelle never liked it when people mispronounced her name "Nellie.") Hohoff's main concern was the structure of *To Kill a Mockingbird*, having recognized that the "editorial call to duty was plain." In her view, Nelle needed "professional help in organizing her material and developing a sound plot structure. After a couple of false starts, the story line, interplay of characters, and fall of emphasis grew clearer, and with each revision—there were many minor changes as the story grew in strength and in Nelle's own vision of it—the true stature of the novel became evident." . . .

Undercutting Nelle's achievement has been a persistent rumor since the book's publication that Truman Capote wrote portions or all of it. "I've heard they were up there at the old Hibbert place, which is right north of Monroeville—out there in the woods," said a former classmate of Nelle's, Claude Nun-

Truman Capote was a childhood friend of Harper Lee and is thought to be the inspiration for the character Dill in To Kill a Mockingbird. *Hulton/Archive.*

nelly. "They just went out there, there's an old farmhouse, and they went out there and wrote and wrote and wrote."

Tay Hohoff's son-in-law, Dr. Grady H. Nunn, said that such a deception wouldn't have occurred to Nelle.

31

I am satisfied that the relationship between Nelle and Tay over those three years while *Mockingbird* was in the making developed into a warmer and closer association than is usual between author and editor. I believe that special association came about at least in part because they worked, together, over every word in the manuscript. Tay and [her husband] Arthur became Nelle's close friends, sort of family, and that friendship continued beyond the publication of the book. I doubt that the special closeness could possibly have happened had there been an alien ghostwriter, Capote, involved.

Also, given Truman's inability to keep anybody's secrets, it's highly unlikely that he wouldn't have claimed right of authorship after the novel became famous. He did say, which Nelle never denied, that he read the manuscript and recommended some edits because it was too long in places.

Without question, however, the hard work of creating *To Kill a Mockingbird* fell squarely on Nelle, though "she always knew I was in her corner," said Hohoff, "even when I was most critical"; and Hohoff was never one to suffer fools gladly, recalled Nicholas Delbanco, another of her young authors. One winter night Nelle was seated at her desk in her apartment on York Avenue, rereading a page in her typewriter over and over. Suddenly she gathered up everything she'd written, walked over to a window, and threw the entire draft outside into the snow. Then she called Hohoff and tearfully explained what she'd done. Tay told her to march outside immediately and pick up the pages. Feeling exhausted, she bundled up and went out into the darkness, "since I knew I could never be happy being anything but a writer . . . I kept at it because I knew it had to be my first novel, for better or for worse."

Nor did the coveted status of being a writer-under-contract change her "intense reserve," as Hohoff called it. She was still shy around strangers, though she could easily have taken out bragging rights on the novel she was writing. "I first met Nelle Lee in 1958," said Dr. Nunn.

We were living in Tuscaloosa, and Tay visited us in connection with a Lippincott-sponsored search for promising authors in the writing program there. There were several such visits during our tenure there. As usual a New York–style cocktail party for Tay was included. Nelle was in Monroeville at the time and was invited up for the party. She arrived, was introduced around, and promptly disappeared. I discovered her later sitting on the back steps with our daughter, who was then five. They were there until Nelle left at the party's end. Definitely Nelle was no party lover.

Besides Hohoff, there were others in her corner, of course. Her second family in Manhattan gathered around her, giving her creative and emotional support. Michael and Joy Brown continued to depend on Nelle as an aunt to their children, and Joy's best friend. Annie Laurie Williams and Maurice Crain [her agent] began inviting Nelle to their summer place, the Old Stone House, in West Hartland, Connecticut, for long weekends. Nelle wrote them long, chatty letters from Monroeville during her visits home, catching them up on family news and local events. One Christmas, she mailed Williams a cowbell as a present, confirming their sisterhood as southern rural people. Another New York agent might have read this gentle overture as a hallmark of someone who was almost embarrassingly unsophisticated. But Williams understood that Nelle was inviting her to become part of her southern family. Then the following year, boughs of fresh-cut Alabama evergreens arrived for the office; Williams reciprocated by sending to Monroeville a box of hard candies because "I remembered you told me that your father loved [them]"; in addition, she promised she was having "some of the farm pictures [of the house in Connecticut] you loved made up for you and they will be along for you to enjoy them with Alice and your father before you leave."

Finally, in the spring of 1959, right before the final draft of the manuscript was ready for delivery to Lippincott, Nelle reached out to a seminal figure in her dream of becoming a writer. She presented her novel to her former English teacher, Miss Gladys Watson, now Mrs. Watson-Burkett, and asked her to critique it. At night, Mrs. Watson-Burkett would take it out of her sewing basket, write notes in the margins, and discuss it with her husband. One day after school, she asked a student, Cecil Ryland, to come up to her desk. According to Ryland, she said she had finished proofreading a novel by a former student, and asked would he please run it over to her house. "And so, I gathered up the manuscript in an old stationery box, and took it and went knocking on her door. Nelle Harper Lee came to the door, and I said, 'Here's your book.' And she said 'Thank you.' Little did I realize that I held a little bit of history in my hands."

Social Issues in Literature

CHAPTER 2

To Kill a Mockingbird and Racism

Southern Values, Old and New

Fred Erisman

Fred Erisman holds a Ph.D. in American studies from the University of Minnesota and taught for thirty-five years at Texas Christian University.

Traditional Southern Romanticism advocates for an "Old South," an outdated sociological structure involving a caste system, class divisions, and sexual taboos. Such a structure leaves those on the periphery—African Americans, poor whites, and women—in subhuman and subordinate conditions.

In To Kill a Mockingbird *Harper Lee promotes a "New South," one based on the Emersonian belief in an ideal spiritual existence. Atticus Finch becomes the personified Emersonian man of the South; it is through the tolerant skepticism and humanity portrayed in Atticus that a new and better South can emerge.*

When Mark Twain stranded the steamboat *Walter Scott* on a rocky point in Chapter 13 of *Huckleberry Finn*, he rounded out an attack on Southern romanticism begun in *Life on the Mississippi*. There, as every reader knows, he asserted that Sir Walter Scott [a Scottish writer active in the early 1800s]'s novels of knighthood and chivalry had done "measureless harm" by infecting the American South with "the jejune romanticism of an absurd past that is dead." This premise does not stop with Twain. W. J. Cash [an American journalist], writing almost sixty years later, continues the assertion, observing that the South, already nostalgic in the early nineteenth century, "found perhaps the most perfect expression for this part of its spirit in the cardboard medievalism of the

Fred Erisman, "The Romantic Regionalism of Harper Lee," *The Alabama Review*, April 1973, pp. 122–131, 133. Copyright © 1973 The University of Alabama Press. All rights reserved. Reproduced by permission.

Scotch novels." As recently as 1961, W. R. Taylor, in *Cavalier and Yankee*, several times alludes to Scott as he traces the development of the myth of the planter aristocracy.

Traditional Southern Romanticism

For these three men, and for many like them, Southern romanticism has been a pernicious, backward-looking belief. It has, they imply, mired the South in a stagnant morass of outdated ideas, from which there is little chance of escape. A more hopeful view, however, appears in Harper Lee's novel of Alabama life, *To Kill a Mockingbird* (1960). Miss Lee is well aware of traditional Southern romanticism and, indeed, agrees that it was and is a pervasive influence in the South; one of the subtlest allusions in the entire novel comes in Chapter 11, as the Finch children read *Ivanhoe* [one of Scott's novels] to the dying but indomitable Southern lady, Mrs. Henry Lafayette Dubose. At the same time, she sees in the New South—the South of 1930–1935—the dawning of a newer and more vital form of romanticism. She does not see this newer romanticism as widespread, nor does she venture any sweeping predictions as to its future. Nevertheless, in *To Kill a Mockingbird*, Miss Lee presents an Emersonian view of Southern romanticism, suggesting that the South can move from the archaic, imported romanticism of its past toward the more reasonable, pragmatic, and native romanticism of a Ralph Waldo Emerson [19th-century American writer and philosopher who as a transcendentalist believed in the existence of an ideal spiritual reality]. If the movement can come to maturity, she implies, the South will have made a major step toward becoming truly regional in its vision.

An Old Town

As Miss Lee unfolds her account of three years in the lives of Atticus, Jem, and Scout Finch, and in the history of Maycomb, Alabama, she makes clear the persistence of the old beliefs.

Maycomb, she says, is "an old town, . . . a tired old town," even "an ancient town." A part of southern Alabama from the time of the first settlements, and isolated and largely untouched by the Civil War, it was, like the South, turned inward upon itself by Reconstruction. Indeed, its history parallels that of the South in so many ways that it emerges as a microcosm of the South. This quality is graphically suggested by the Maycomb County courthouse, which dominates the town square:

> The Maycomb County courthouse was faintly reminiscent of Arlington in one respect: the concrete pillars supporting its south roof were too heavy for their light burden. The pillars were all that remained standing when the original courthouse burned in 1856. Another courthouse was built around them. It is better to say, built in spite of them. But for the south porch, the Maycomb County courthouse was early Victorian, presenting an unoffensive vista when seen from the north. From the other side, however, Greek revival columns clashed with a big nineteenth-century clock tower housing a rusty unreliable instrument, a view indicating a people determined to preserve every physical scrap of the past.

Miss Lee's courthouse, inoffensive from the north but architecturally appalling from the south, neatly summarizes Maycomb's reluctance to shed the past. It is, like the South, still largely subject to the traditions of the past.

The microcosmic quality of Maycomb suggested by its courthouse appears in other ways, as well. The town's social structure, for example, is characteristically Southern. Beneath its deceptively placid exterior, Maycomb has a taut, well-developed caste system designed to separate whites from blacks. If Maycomb's caste system is not so openly oppressive as that of John Dollard's "Southerntown" (where "caste has replaced slavery as a means of maintaining the essence of the old status order in the South"), it still serves the same end—to keep the blacks in their place. The operations of this system

Gregory Peck played Atticus Finch in the film adaptation of To Kill a Mockingbird *and won the Academy Award for Best Actor in 1962.* Hulton Archive/Getty Images.

are obvious. First Purchase African M. E. Church, for example, "the only church in Maycomb with a steeple and bell," is subjected to minor but consistent desecration: "Negroes worshiped in it on Sundays and white men gambled in it on weekdays." The whites, moreover, clearly expect deferential behavior of the blacks. One of the good ladies of the Methodist missionary circle interrupts her paeans to Christian fellowship to remark, "There's nothing more distracting than a sulky darky. . . . Just ruins your day to have one of 'em in the kitchen." The Finch children, attending church with Calpurnia, their black housekeeper, are confronted with doffed hats and "weekday gestures of respectful attention." And, in the most telling commentary of all upon the pervasive pressures of the caste system, when Calpurnia accompanies Atticus Finch to convey the news of Tom Robinson's death, she must ride in the back seat of the automobile.

Sexual Taboos and Aristocracy

Even more indicative of Maycomb's characteristically Southern caste system is the power of the sexual taboo, which has been called "the strongest taboo of the system." This is dramatized by the maneuverings during Tom Robinson's trial of allegedly raping Mayella Ewell, a central episode in the novel. Although Tom's infraction of the black man–white woman code is demonstrated to have been false, he is nonetheless condemned. The caste taboo outweighs empirical evidence. As Atticus says later of the jury, "Those are twelve reasonable men in everyday life, Tom's jury, but you saw something come between them and reason. . . . There's something in our world that makes men lose their heads—they couldn't be fair if they tried." Despite the presence of a more than reasonable doubt as to his guilt, despite the discrediting of the Ewells, the chief witnesses for the prosecution, Tom Robinson is condemned. As Atticus points out, the entire prosecution is based upon "the assumption—the evil assumption—that *all* Negroes lie, that *all* Negroes are basically immoral beings, that *all* Negro men are not to be trusted around our women." Tom's conviction is mute testimony to the strength of that caste-oriented assumption.

Another illustration of Maycomb's archetypal Southernness that is as typical as its caste system is the ubiquitous system of class distinctions among the whites. Miss Lee's characters fall readily into four classes, ranging from the "old aristocracy" represented by Atticus Finch's class-conscious sister, Alexandra, to the poor white trash represented by Bob Ewell and his brood, who have been "the disgrace of Maycomb for three generations." In presenting the interaction of these classes, she gives a textbook demonstration of the traditional social stratification of the American South.

The upper-class-consciousness so manifest in Aunt Alexandra appears most strongly in her regard for "family," a concern that permeates Part II of *To Kill a Mockingbird*. Like the small-town aristocrats described in Allison Davis's *Deep South*, she has a keen appreciation of the "laterally extended kin group." Although the complex interrelationships of Maycomb society are generally known to the Finch children, it is Aunt Alexandra who drives home their social significance. After a series of social gaffes by Scout, Aunt Alexandra prevails upon Atticus to lecture the children concerning their status. This he does, in his most inflectionless manner:

> Your aunt has asked me to try and impress upon you and Jean Louise that you are not from run-of-the-mill people, that you are the product of several generations' gentle breeding . . . and that you should try to live up to your name. . . . She asked me to tell you you must try to behave like the little lady and gentleman that you are. She wants to talk to you about the family and what it's meant to Maycomb County through the years, so you'll have some idea of who you are, so you might be moved to behave accordingly.

In her insistence that family status be perserved, Aunt Alexandra typifies the family-oriented aristocrat of the Old South.

Class Distinctions

No less well developed is Miss Lee's emphasis upon the subtleties of class distinction. In this, too, she defines Maycomb as a characteristically Southern community. It has its upper class, in Aunt Alexandra, in the members of the Missionary Society, and in the town's professional men—Atticus, Dr. Reynolds, Judge Taylor, and so on. It has its middle class, in the numerous faceless and often nameless individuals who flesh out Miss Lee's story—Braxton Underwood, the owner-editor of *The Maycomb Tribune*, or Mr. Sam Levy, who shamed the Ku Klux Klan in 1920 by proclaiming that "he'd sold 'em the very sheets on their backs." It has its lower class, generically condemned by Aunt Alexandra as "trash," but sympathetically presented in characters like Walter Cunningham, one of the Cunninghams of Old Sarum, a breed of men who "hadn't taken anything from or off of anybody since they migrated to the New World." Finally, it has its dregs, the Ewells, who, though more slovenly than the supposedly slovenliest of the blacks, still possess the redeeming grace of a white skin. These distinctions Aunt Alexandra reveres and protects, as when she remarks, "You can scrub Walter Cunningham till he shines, you can put him in shoes and a new suit, but he'll never be like Jem. . . . Because—he—is—trash." For Aunt Alexandra, the class gap between the Finches and the Cunninghams is one that can never be bridged.

The existence of a caste system separating black from white, or of a well-developed regard for kin-group relations, or of a system of class stratification is, of course, not unique. But, from the simultaneous existence of these three systems, and from the way in which they dominate Maycomb attitudes, emerges the significance of Maycomb's antiquity. It is a representation of the Old South, still clinging, as in its courthouse, to every scrap of the past. Left alone, it would remain static, moldering away as surely as John Brown's body [17th-century abolitionist who was hanged after leading an unsuccessful raid at Harper's Ferry, VA]. So too, Miss Lee suggests, may the South. This decay however, can be prevented. In her picture of the New South and the New Southerner, Miss Lee suggests how a decadently romantic tradition can be transformed into a functional romanticism, and how, from this change, can come a revitalizing of the South.

The New South

The "New South" that Harper Lee advocates is new only by courtesy. In one respect—the degree to which it draws upon the romantic idealism of an Emerson—it is almost as old as the Scottish novels so lacerated by Mark Twain; in another, it is even older, as it at times harks back to the Puritan ideals of the seventeenth century. By the standards of the American South of the first third of the twentieth century, however, it is new, for it flies in the face of much that traditionally characterizes the South. With Emerson, it spurns the past, looking instead to the reality of the present. With him, it places principled action above self-interest, willingly accepting the difficult consequences of a right decision. It recognizes, like both Emerson and the Puritans, the diversity of mankind, yet recognizes also that this diversity is unified by a set of "higher laws" that cannot be ignored. In short, in the several Maycomb townspeople who see through the fog of the past, and who act not from tradition but from principle, Miss Lee presents the possible salvation of the South.

Foremost among these people is Atticus Finch, attorney, the central character of Miss Lee's novel. Though himself a native of Maycomb, a member of one of the oldest families in the area, and "related by blood or marriage to nearly every family in the town," Atticus is not the archetypal Southerner that his sister has become. Instead, he is presented as a Southern version of Emersonian man, the individual who vibrates to his own iron string, the one man in the town that the community trusts "to do right," even as they deplore his peculiarities. Through him, and through Jem and Scout, the children he is rearing according to his lights, Miss Lee presents her view of the New South.

Atticus's Tolerant Skepticism

That Atticus Finch is meant to be an atypical Southerner is plain; Miss Lee establishes this from the beginning, as she reports that Atticus and his brother are the first Finches to leave the family lands and study elsewhere. This atypical quality, however, is developed even further. Like Emerson, Atticus recognizes that his culture is retrospective, groping "among the dry bones of the past . . . [and putting] the living generation into masquerade out of its faded wardrobe." He had no hostility toward his past; he is not one of the alienated souls so beloved of Southern Gothicists [a group of writers, including

Flannery O'Connor and William Faulkner, who set supernatural tales in the South]. He does, though, approach his past and its traditions with a tolerant skepticism. His attitude toward "old family" and "gentle breeding" has already been suggested. A similar skepticism is implied by his repeated observation that "you never really understand a person until you consider things from his point of view . . . until you climb into his skin and walk around in it." He understands the difficulties of Tom Robinson, although Tom Robinson is black; he understands the difficulties of a Walter Cunningham, though Cunningham is—to Aunt Alexandra—"trash"; he understands the pressures being brought to bear upon his children because of his own considered actions. In each instance he acts according to his estimate of the merits of the situation, striving to see that each receives justice. He is, in short, as Edwin Bruell has suggested, "no heroic type but any graceful, restrained, simple person like one from Attica." Unfettered by the corpse of the past, he is free to live and work as an individual.

This freedom to act he does not gain easily. Indeed, he, like Emerson's nonconformist, frequently finds himself whipped by the world's displeasure. And yet, like Emerson's ideal man, when faced by this harassment and displeasure, he has "the habit of magnanimity and religion to treat it godlike as a trifle of no concernment." In the development of this habit he is aided by a strong regard for personal principle, even as he recognizes the difficulty that it brings to his life and the lives of his children. This is established early in the novel, with the introduction of the Tom Robinson trial. When the case is brought up by Scout, following a fight at school, Atticus responds, "'If I didn't [defend Tom Robinson] I couldn't hold up my head in town, I couldn't represent this county in the legislature, I couldn't even tell you or Jem not to do something again. . . . Scout, simply by the nature of the work, every lawyer gets at least one case in his lifetime that affects him personally. This one's mine, I guess.'" He returns to this theme later, observing that "'This case . . . is something that goes to the essence of a man's conscience—Scout, I couldn't go to church and worship God if I didn't try to help that man.'" Scout points out that opinion among the townspeople runs counter to this, whereupon Atticus replies, "'They're certainly entitled to think that, and they're entitled to full respect for their opinions . . . but before I can live with other folks I've got to live with myself. The one thing that doesn't abide by majority rule is a person's conscience.'" No careful ear is needed to hear the echoes of Emerson's "Nothing can bring you peace but yourself. Nothing can bring you peace but the triumph of principles." In his heeding both principle and conscience, whatever the cost to himself, Atticus is singularly Emersonian. . . .

Exchanging Old for New

Throughout *To Kill a Mockingbird*, Harper Lee presents a dual view of the American South. On the one hand, she sees the South as still in the grip of [its old] traditions and habits . . . caste division along strictly color lines, hierarchical class stratification within castes, and exaggerated regard for kin-group relations within particular classes, especially the upper and middle classes of the white caste. On the other hand, she argues that the South has within itself the potential for progressive change, stimulated by the incorporation of the New England romanticism of an Emerson, and characterized by the pragmatism, principles, and wisdom of Atticus Finch. If, as she suggests, the South can exchange its old romanticism for the new, it can modify its life to bring justice and humanity to all of its inhabitants, black and white alike.

The Case Against
To Kill a Mockingbird

Isaac Saney

Isaac Saney is a faculty member at Dalhousie University and Saint Mary's University, both in Halifax, Canada. He has published many articles on the theme of race and racism.

In an attempt to censor To Kill a Mockingbird, *the Black Educators' Association cited the book's language and stereotyping of blacks as primary reasons it needed to be banned from Canadian schools. The use of the word "Nigger" (used forty-eight times in the novel) as well as the portrayal of blacks as "innocent" mockingbirds, they purported, only further spread racism in today's youth. Saney concurred and further objected to what he called the book's historically inaccurate message—seen through the defense of black Tom Robinson by white Atticus Finch—that whites, instead of blacks, led the antiracist movement of the twentieth century.*

For many years the Black Educators' Association and parents, amongst others, have lobbied the Nova Scotia Department of Education and school boards to remove various books from the school curriculum and school use. Similar initiatives have taken place in New Brunswick and other provinces across Canada. Pressure from the community forced the Department of Education to face up to its social responsibility to provide enlightened education and teaching materials and address the issue of restricting racist materials in the province's classrooms, in the same way that pressure had forced the government to abandon its legislated policy of segregated schooling for the African Nova Scotian population, a policy only

formally ended in the 1950s. In 1996, after intensive community pressure, three works—*To Kill a Mockingbird* by Harper
Lee; *In the Heat of the Night* by John Dudley Ball; and *Under-
ground to Canada* by Barbara Smucker—were taken off the
authorised list of texts recommended by the Department of
Education. They can no longer be purchased from the provincial government.

Six years later, in March 2002, the African Nova Scotian ad
hoc advisory committee (a committee of parents and
educators) of the Tri-County district, which runs schools in
southwestern Nova Scotia, recommended that the three works
should be removed from school use altogether. Many educators consider these demands as minimal and as barely beginning to address the serious inequalities which continue to per-
vade the education system. Members of the Black Educators'
Association (BEA) again seconded this specific recommendation. In the words of BEA director Gerry Clarke, a former
school principal: 'It's demeaning and offensive to those students who have to put up with this.' Indeed, a 2000 report on
To Kill a Mockingbird laid out the community's concerns:

> In this novel, African Canadian students are presented with
> language that portrays all the stereotypical generalizations
> that demean them as a people. While the white student and
> white teacher may misconstrue it as language of an earlier
> era or the way it was, this language is still widely used today
> and the book serves as a tool to reinforce its usage even fur-
> ther ... The terminology in this novel subjects students to
> humiliating experiences that rob them of their self-respect
> and the respect of their peers. The word 'Nigger' is used
> forty-eight times [in] the novel ... There are many available
> books which reflect the past history of African-Canadians or
> Americans without subjecting African-Canadian learners to
> this type of degradation ... We believe that the English Lan-
> guage Arts curriculum in Nova Scotia must enable all stu-
> dents to feel comfortable with ideas, feelings and experi-
> ences presented without fear of humiliation ... *To Kill a*

> *Mockingbird* is clearly a book that no longer meets these
> goals and therefore must no longer be used for classroom
> instruction.[1]

The recommendation to remove the books was initially
agreed to by the Tri-County School Board which ordered the
works removed from school use in Shelburne, Yarmouth and
Digby counties. However, pandemonium broke loose all over
the printed press, radio and television media, nationally and
internationally. In the main Canadian and provincial newspapers, some twenty-eight articles appeared. When the educators
explained that the works used abusive and racist language and
perpetuated demeaning stereotypical images and generalisa-
tions, emphasising that the books did not meet the needs of
'all students', the Canadian monopoly-controlled news media
immediately took what had been said out of context and declared that the Black community had embraced 'book banning'
and 'censorship'. Opposition to the books, especially *To Kill a
Mockingbird*, was likened to 'the gathering shadow of
oppression'.[2] Thus, the media gave far more coverage to this
distortion than to the substance of the Black community's
recommendations.

The *National Post* [based out of Toronto, Ontario, Canada]
went so far as to survey such leading American literary figures
as Chicago Mayor Richard Daley on the merits of *To Kill a
Mockingbird*, citing its use in city-wide reading contests 'as
springboards for citywide discussions' for its 'message of acceptance [of] people of other races than your own'. It then argued, how could Nova Scotia have a different policy to the
United States, asserting that '[t]here are more blacks in Chicago than there are people in Nova Scotia'.[3] An accompanying
editorial declared that racism was a matter of the past and
blamed 'the anti-racism industry' for obscuring the 'historical
content in which overt racism once thrived'.[4] *National Post*
columnist Robert Fulford likewise converted the recommendation that the book not be used by teachers in the classroom

into a call to ban the 'much-loved book' and fulminated how those who had been oppressed were now calling for 'censorship' 'for the sole reason that they [the books] contain this intolerable word ("Nigger")'. Referring to comments by the BEA's Brenda Clarke, he declared: 'Beware of those who believe they can manage the self-esteem of others by denying them books. She demonstrates that the impulse to censor never dies, it just changes targets.'[5] The [Toronto] *Globe and Mail* in its editorial, published on the same day and under the identical title as the *National Post*'s, termed Harper Lee's book a 'wonderful teaching tool' and also called for Canadians to emulate Chicago, which 'felt it would encourage greater racial understanding'.[6] Consequently, after the media frenzy and the intervention of the minister of education, Jane Purves, the Tri-County school board changed its stand on 30 May 2002 in a 6-2 vote.

The arguments advanced by the Black community were consistently presented in a non-serious, even risible, light so as to give the impression that the Black educators and parents are ignorant of the merits of literature, mere emotional whiners and complainers, belonging to a hot-headed fringe. For example, after the decision was made to keep books in the curriculum, the *Halifax Daily News* [Halifax is the capital of Nova Scotia] in an editorial was 'relieved cooler heads have prevailed', reproducing the racist notions of inherent Black emotionality versus rationality of white society.[7]

To Kill a Mockingbird

Editorialists were especially incensed that *To Kill a Mockingbird* had come under criticism. The book was lauded as a classic, a paragon of anti-racist literature and, therefore, untouchable and sacrosanct.[8] The Black community was chided for being overly sensitive to the use of racial slurs and for its failure [to] appreciate the context and message of the novel. What was ignored was that the use of racist epithets or negative and debased imagery is not the only basis upon which to determine the racist or anti-racist character of a book. Jane Kansas, a columnist for the *Halifax Daily News*, typified the prevailing mindset. She, along with other partisans of the book, invoked the lecture Miss Maudie Atkinson delivers to Atticus Finch's daughter, Scout, on why it is 'a sin to kill a mockingbird'. This 'homily' was extolled as the most eloquent literary anti-racist statement.[9] Indeed, the lines define the book:

> 'Mockingbirds don't do one thing but make music for us to enjoy. They don't eat up people's gardens, don't nest in corncribs, they don't do one thing but sing their hearts out for us. That's why it's a sin to kill a mockingbird.'[10]

However, Kansas and others failed to explore the obvious meaning behind these words. Is not the mockingbird a metaphor for the entire African American population? Do these lines, as the partisans of the book assert, embody the loftiest ideals and sentiments? Harper Lee's motives notwithstanding, they are not a paean [a song of praise] to the intrinsic equality and humanity of all peoples, nor do they acknowledge that Blacks are endowed with the same worth and rights as whites. What these lines *say* is that Black people are useful and harmless creatures akin to decorous pets—that should not be treated brutally. This is reminiscent of the thinking that pervaded certain sectors of the abolition movement against slavery which did not extol the equality of Africans, but paralleled the propaganda of the Society for the Prevention of Cruelty to Animals, arguing that just as one should not treat one's horse, ox or dog cruelly, one should not treat one's Black cruelly.[11] By foisting this mockingbird image on African Americans, the novel does not challenge the insidious conception of superior versus inferior 'races', the notion of those meant to rule versus those meant to be ruled. What it attacks are the worst—particularly violent—excesses of the racist social order, leaving the racist social order itself intact. In short, as Malcolm X would probably have said, it presents the outlook of the 'enlightened' versus the 'unenlightened' slave owner, who wishes to preserve the value of his human property, the beasts of burden, to labour for his benefit, enjoyment and profit.

Central to the view that *To Kill a Mockingbird* is a solid and inherently anti-racist work is the role of Atticus Finch, the white lawyer who defends Tom Robinson, the Black man wrongly accused of raping a white woman. Indeed, Atticus goes so far as to save Tom from a lynching.[12] However, this act has no historical foundation. The acclaimed exhibition Without Sanctuary: Lynching Photography in America, sponsored by the Roth-Horowitz Gallery and the New York Historical Society, documented more than six hundred incidents of lynching. This landmark exposition and study established that 'lynchers tended to be ordinary people and respectable people, few of whom had any difficulties justifying their atrocities in the name of maintaining the social and racial order and the purity of the Anglo-Saxon race'.[13] In two years of investigation, the exhibit researchers found no evidence of intervention by a white person to stop even a single lynching.

Perhaps the most egregious characteristic of the novel is the denial of the historical agency of Black people. They are robbed of their role as subjects of history, reduced to mere objects who are passive hapless victims; mere spectators and bystanders in the struggle against their own oppression and exploitation. There's the rub! The novel and its supporters deny that Black people have been the central actors in their movement for liberation and justice, from widespread African resistance to, and revolts against, slavery and colonialism to the twentieth century's mass movements challenging segregation, discrimination and imperialism. Yet, *To Kill a Mockingbird* confounds the relationship between whites of conscience and the struggles of the Black community. The novel is set in the 1930s and portrays Blacks as somnolent [sleepy, inactive], awaiting someone from outside to take up and fight for the cause of justice. It is as if the Scottsboro case—in which nine young Black men travelling on a freight train in search of work were wrongfully convicted of raping two white women who were riding the same freight train—never happened. The trial was a 'legal lynching carried through with the cooperation of the courts and the law enforcement agencies'.[14] All but one were sentenced to death; the jury was hung on whether the ninth one should be sentenced to life imprisonment or death. The germane [relevant] point is that a maelstrom of activity swept through African-American communities, both North and South. They organised, agitated, petitioned and marched in support of and to free the nine young men. *To Kill a Mockingbird* gives no inkling of this mass protest and instead creates the indelible impression that the entire Black community existed in a complete state of paralysis. It was African North Americans who took up the task of confronting and organising against racism, who through weal and woe, trial and tribulation, carried on—and still carry on the battle for equal rights and dignity. Those whites who did, and do, make significant contributions gave, and give, their solidarity in response.

However, this necessary historical contextualisation for dealing adequately with the book rarely occurs in the classroom. Thus, the images and messages of *To Kill a Mockingbird* are given new life, despite the reality that—as in the case of *Uncle Tom's Cabin*—these motifs have long since outlived any positive and progressive purpose and are not only useless for today's task of building a society based on true equality, but, indeed, are a detriment and a retrogressive block. Furthermore, there has been considerable resistance to the incorporation of available literature reflecting both the African American and African Nova Scotian experience. Repeated suggestions have been made to include in the curriculum, for example, *In-*

visible Man by Ralph Ellison; *Native Son* by Richard Wright; *Their Eyes Were Watching God* by Zora Neale Hurston; *The Autobiography of Malcolm X; Beloved* and *The Bluest Eye* by Toni Morrison; *Whylah Falls* by George Elliot Clarke and *Consecrated Ground* by George Boyd. The last two authors are award-winning Black Nova Scotians. Indeed, Clarke was the 2002 recipient of Canada's most prestigious literary prize, the Governor General's Award.

Conclusion

The hardworking and humble educators and parents, selfless volunteer contributors of their time and energies, who made these recommendations honestly and honourably, had to contend with the stigma of being called 'benign censors' as they were shamelessly branded. Their well-reasoned and reasonable opposition, based on a clear and sound understanding of history and education, was caricatured and demeaned. The dominant media, within and without Nova Scotia, affirmed that the degrading portrayal of an entire people, the continual depiction of servitude and the negation of historical agency are the hallmarks of classic literature. What prevailed were the outdated ideas of the nineteenth century, affinity and devotion to paternalistic conceptions of society; a reflection of the imbalance of power and marginalisation embedded in the status quo.

In short, the media's response amounted to a defence of 'freedom' for racist literature. The issue cannot be reduced to a matter of technical arguments and justifications or the advocating of a parallel 'anti-racist' curriculum. The racists today masquerade as 'anti-racists', the opponents of 'hate literature'. The media's editorialising against all 'censorship' and 'banning' includes vigorous hostility to the censorship and banning of racism. Its advocacy of freedom of speech includes freedom of speech for racists and fascists. There cannot be the slightest mystery about how racism works, particularly its intertwining with the state. Neither fully curable nor manageable in the present social order, racism cannot be tackled at leisure; it must be combated in all its forms, without pause. However, in this struggle educators and writers must not forget that they are not dealing with an honourable media; that dirty and ruthless political warfare is being waged over the question of racism on the front of literature and ideology.

Notes

1. 'A proposal regarding the usage of the novel: *To Kill a Mockingbird*' (Halifax, African-Canadian Services Division, Nova Scotia Department of Education and the Race Relations Coordinators in Nova Scotia, English program division of the Education Department, February 4, 2000).
2. Jane Kansas, 'Censors Would Kill Mockingbird's Song'. *Daily News* (5 May 2002).
3. Anne Marie Owens, 'U.S. Embraces Novel N.S. Group Wants Ban', *National Post* (7 May 2002).
4. 'To Ban a Mockingbird', *National Post* (7 May 2002).
5. Robert Fulford, 'We Have to Believe Reason Beats Racism', *National Post* (11 May 2002).
6. 'To Ban a Mockingbird'. *Globe & Mail* (7 May 2002).
7. 'Cooler Heads Prevail over Ban', *Daily News* (9 May 2002).
8. 'Novel Dilemma', *Chronicle Herald* (12 May 2002).
9. Jane Kansas, op. cit.
10. Harper Lee. *To Kill a Mockingbird* (London, Pan, 1981), p. 96.
11. See comment by Richard Hart in the documentary 'The Black Image: Representations of Africans in Europe throughout History' (London, Association for Curriculum Development, 1990).
12. Lee, op. cit., p. 154: 8.
13. See James Allen and Leon F. Litwack, *Without Sanctuary: Lynching Photography in America* (Sante Fe, NM, Twin Palms. 2000).
14. Harry Haywood. *Black Bolshevik: Autobiography of an Afro-American Communist* (Chicago, Liberator Press, 1978).

In Defense of
To Kill a Mockingbird

Jill May

Jill May is a professor of literacy and language at Purdue University.

Literary critic Theo D'Haen believes good literature should have "life within the world." Author Jill May agrees, although she understands how this makes some literature difficult to face. This is the case of To Kill a Mockingbird. *The "life" represented in the novel contributes to the harsh criticism it has received, as there is an unwillingness to face the grimness of this moment in American history.*

Published in 1960, To Kill a Mockingbird *has received criticism from conservatives and liberals alike. While conservatives claim the book poorly portrays whites, liberals find racist elements within the words and context. In contrast, May celebrates the novel's truthfulness in telling Americans what they would rather not hear, because only in doing so can readers prepare to meet life's realities.*

The critical career of *To Kill a Mockingbird* is a late-twentieth-century case study of censorship. When Harper Lee's novel about a small southern town and its prejudices was published in 1960, the book received favorable reviews in professional journals and the popular press. Typical of that opinion, *Booklist*'s reviewer called the book "melodramatic" and noted "traces of sermonizing," but the book was recommended for library purchase, commending its "rare blend of wit and compassion." Reviewers did not suggest that the book was young adult literature, or that it belonged in adolescent collections; perhaps that is why no one mentioned the book's language or violence. In any event, reviewers seemed inclined to agree that *To Kill a Mockingbird* was a worthwhile interpretation of the South's existing social structures during the 1930s. In 1961 the book won the Pulitzer Prize Award, the Alabama Library Association Book Award, and the Brotherhood Award of the National Conference of Christians and Jews. It seemed that Harper Lee's blend of family history, local custom, and restrained sermonizing was important reading, and with a young girl between the ages of six and nine as the main character, *To Kill a Mockingbird* moved rapidly into junior and senior high school libraries and curriculum. The book was not destined to be studied by college students. Southern literature's critics rarely mentioned it; few university professors found it noteworthy enough to "teach" as an exemplary southern novel.

Criticism of *To Kill a Mockingbird*

By the mid-sixties *To Kill a Mockingbird* had a solid place in junior and senior high American literature studies. Once discovered by southern parents, the book's solid place became shaky indeed. Sporadic lawsuits arose. In most cases the complaint against the book was by conservatives who disliked the portrayal of whites. Typically, the Hanover County School Board in Virginia first ruled the book "immoral," then withdrew their criticism and declared that the ruckus "was all a mistake". By 1968 the National Education Association listed the book among those which drew the most criticism from private groups. Ironically it was rated directly behind *Little Black Sambo*. And then the seventies arrived.

Things had changed in the South during the sixties. Two national leaders who had supported integration and had espoused the ideals of racial equality were assassinated in southern regions. When John F. Kennedy was killed in Texas on

November 22, 1963, many southerners were shocked. Populist attitudes of racism were declining, and in the aftermath of the tragedy southern politics began to change. Lyndon Johnson gained the presidency; blacks began to seek and win political offices. Black leader Martin Luther King had stressed the importance of racial equality, always using Mahatma Gandhi's strategy of nonviolent action and civil disobedience. A brilliant orator, King grew up in the South; the leader of the Southern Christian Leadership Conference, he lived in Atlanta, Georgia. In 1968, while working on a garbage strike in Memphis, King was killed. The death of this 1965 Nobel Peace Prize winner was further embarrassment for white southerners. Whites began to look at public values anew, and gradually southern blacks found experiences in the South more tolerable. In 1971 one Atlanta businessman observed in *Ebony*, "The liberation thinking is here. Blacks are more together. With the doors opening wider, this area is the mecca. . . ." Southern arguments against *To Kill a Mockingbird* subsided. *The Newsletter on Intellectual Freedom* contained no record of southern court cases during the seventies or eighties. The book had sustained itself during the first period of sharp criticism; it had survived regional protests from the area it depicted.

The second onslaught of attack came from new groups of censors, and it came during the late seventies and early eighties. Private sectors in the Midwest and suburban East began to demand the book's removal from school libraries. Groups, such as the Eden Valley School Committee in Minnesota, claimed that the book was too laden with profanity. In Vernon, New York, Reverend Carl Hadley threatened to establish a private Christian school because public school libraries contained such "filthy, trashy sex novels" as *A Separate Peace* and *To Kill a Mockingbird*. And finally, blacks began to censor the book. In Warren, Indiana, three black parents resigned from the township Human Relations Advisory Council when the

Warren County school administration refused to remove the book from Warren junior high school classes. They contended that the book "does psychological damage to the positive integration process and represents institutionalized racism". Thus, censorship of *To Kill a Mockingbird* swung from the conservative right to the liberal left. Factions representing racists, religious sects, concerned parents and minority groups vocally demanded the book's removal from public schools. With this kind of offense, what makes *To Kill a Mockingbird* worth defending and keeping?

Setting of *To Kill a Mockingbird*

When Harper Lee first introduces Scout in *To Kill a Mockingbird*, she is almost six years old. By the end of the book Scout is in the third grade. Throughout the book events are described by the adult Scout who looks back upon life in the constricted society of a small southern town. Since it is the grown-up Scout's story, the young Scout Finch becomes a memory more than a reality. The book is not a vivid recollection of youth gone by so much as a recounting of days gone by. Yet, Scout Finch's presence as the events' main observer establishes two codes of honor, that of the child and of the adult. The code of adult behavior shows the frailty of adult sympathy for humanity and emphasizes its subsequent effect upon overt societal attitudes. Throughout the book Scout sees adults accepting society's rules rather than confronting them. When Scout finds school troublesome, Atticus tells Scout that they will continue reading together at night, then adds, "you'd better not say anything at school about our agreement." He explains away the Maycomb Ku Klux Klan, saying, "it was a political organization more than anything. Besides, they couldn't find anybody to scare." And when he discusses the case of a black man's word against a white man's with his brother, Atticus says, "The jury couldn't possibly be expected to take Tom Robinson's word against the Ewells' . . . Why reasonable people go stark raving mad when anything involving a Negro comes up, is something I don't pretend to understand." The author tells us that Atticus knew Scout was listening in on this conversation and purposely explained that he had been court appointed, adding, "I'd hoped to get through life without a case of this kind. . . ." And when the jury does see fit to try and condemn Tom Robinson, Scout's older brother Jem and good friend Dill see the white southern world for what it is: a world of hypocrisy, a world burdened with old racist attitudes which have nothing to do with humanity. Jem says, "I always thought Maycomb folks were the best folks in the world, least that's what they seemed like." Dill decides he will be a new kind of clown. "I'm gonna stand in the middle of the ring and laugh at the folks. . . . Every one of 'em oughta be ridin' broomsticks."

The majority of white adults in Maycomb are content to keep blacks, women, and children in their place. Atticus's only sister comes to live with the family and constantly tells Scout she must learn how to act, that she has a place in society: womanhood with its stifling position of prim behavior and wagging tongues is the essence of southern decorum. Even Atticus, the liberal-minded hero, says that perhaps it's best to keep women off the juries of Alabama because, "I doubt if we'd ever get a complete case tried—the ladies'd be interrupting to ask questions." By the end of the book Scout has accepted the rules of southern society. The once hated aunt who insisted upon Scout's transformation into a proper young lady becomes an idol for her ability to maintain proper deportment during a crisis. Scout follows suit, reasoning "if Aunty could be a lady at a time like this, so could I."

Southern Justice

The courtroom trial is a real example of Southern justice and Southern local color storytelling. Merrill Skaggs has analyzed the local color folklore of southern trials in his book *The Folk*

In an infamous case of racism that took place during Harper Lee's youth, several African Americans were falsely accused of raping two white girls in Scottsboro, Alabama and only let free after years of struggle. Heavily covered in the news, the case may have influenced To Kill a Mockingbird. *Hulton Archive/Getty Images.*

of Southern Fiction. Skaggs comments that there is a formula for court hearings, and he suggests that local color stories show that justice in the courtroom is, in fact, less fair than justice in the streets. He discusses justice in terms of the black defendant, saying, "Implicit in these stories . . . is an admission that Negroes are not usually granted equal treatment before the law, that a Negro is acquitted only when he has a white champion." During the trial in *To Kill a Mockingbird* Tom Robinson says he ran because he feared southern justice. He ran, he says, because he was "scared I'd hafta face up to what I didn't do." Dill is one of Lee's young protagonists. He is angered by the southern court system. The neglected son of an itinerant mother, Dill is a stereotype of southern misfits. Lee doesn't concentrate upon Dill's background; she concentrates upon his humanity. The courtroom scene is more than local humor to him. It is appalling. When he flees the trial, Scout follows. She cannot understand why Dill is upset, but the notorious rich "drunk" with "mixed children" can. He sees Dill and says, "it just makes you sick, doesn't it?" No one, save Jem and his youthful converts, expects Atticus to win. The black minister who has befriended the children warns, "I ain't ever seen any jury decide in favor of a colored man over a white man." In the end Atticus says, "They've done it before and they did it tonight and they'll do it again and when they do it—seems that only children weep." And Miss Maudie tells the children, "as I waited I thought, Atticus Finch won't win, he can't win, but he's the only man in these parts who can keep a jury out so long in a case like that." Then she adds, "we're making a step—it's just a baby-step, but it's a step."

In his book, Skaggs points out that obtaining justice through the law is not as important as the courtroom play in southern trials and that because the courtroom drama seldom brings real justice, people condone "violence within the community." Atticus realizes that "justice" is often resolved outside of the court, and so he is not surprised when the sheriff and the town leaders arrive at his house one night. The men warn Atticus that something might happen to Tom Robinson if he is left in the local jail; the sheriff suggests that he can't be responsible for any violence which might occur. One of the men says, "—don't see why you touched it [the case] in the first place. . . . You've got everything to lose from this, Atticus. I mean everything." Because Atticus wants courtroom justice to resolve this conflict, he tries to protect his client. On the night before the trial Atticus moves to the front of the jail, armed only with his newspaper. While there, the local lynching society arrives, ready to take justice into its own hands. Scout, Jem, and Dill have been watching in their own dark corner, but the crowd bothers Scout and so she bursts from her hiding spot. As she runs by, Scout smells "stale whiskey and pigpen," and she realizes that these are not the same men who came to the house earlier. It is Scout's innocence, her misinterpretation of the seriousness of the scene, her ability to recognize one of the farmers and to talk with guileless ease to that man about his own son which saves Tom Robinson from being lynched. The next morning Jem suggests that the men would have killed Atticus if Scout hadn't come along. Atticus, who is more familiar with adult southern violence, says "might have hurt me a little, but son, you'll understand folks a little better when you're older. A mob's always made up of people; no matter what. . . . Every little mob in every little southern town is always made up of people you know—doesn't say much for them does it?" Lynching is a part of regional lore in the South. In his study of discrimination, Wallace Mendelson pointed out that the frequency of lynchings as settlement for black/white problems is less potent than the terrorizing aspect of hearing about them. In this case, the terrorizing aspect of mob rule had been viewed by the children. Its impact would remain.

Southern "Honor"

After the trial Bob Ewell is subjected to a new kind of Southern justice, a polite justice. Atticus explains, "He thought he'd be a hero, but all he got for his pain . . . was, okay; we'll convict this Negro but get back to your dump." Ewell spits on Atticus, cuts a hole in the judge's screen, and harasses Tom's wife. Atticus ignores his insults and figures, "He'll settle down when the weather changes." Scout and Jem never doubt that Ewell is serious, and they are afraid. Their early childhood experiences with the violence and hypocrisy in southern white society have taught them not to trust Atticus's reasoning but they resolve to hide their fear from the adults around them. When Ewell does strike for revenge, he strikes at children. The sheriff understands this kind of violence. It is similar to lynching violence. It strikes at a minority who cannot strike back, and it creates a terror in law-abiding citizens more potent than courtroom justice. It shows that southern honor has been consistently dealt with outside of the courtroom.

Harper Lee's book concerns the behavior of Southerners in their claim for "honor," and Boo Radley's presence in the story reinforces that claim. When Boo was young and got into trouble, his father claimed the right to protect his family name. He took his son home and kept him at the house. When Boo attacked him, Mr. Radley again asked for family privilege; Boo was returned to his home, this time never to surface on the porch or in the yard during the daylight hours. The children are fascinated with the Boo Radley legend. They act it out, and they work hard to make Boo come out. And always, they wonder what keeps him inside. After the trial however, Jem says, "I think I'm beginning to understand something. I think I'm beginning to understand why Boo Radley's stayed shut up in the house . . . it's because he *wants* to stay inside."

Throughout the book Boo is talked about and wondered over, but he does not appear in Scout's existence until the end when he is needed by the children. When no one is near to protect them from death, Boo comes out of hiding. In an act of violence he kills Bob Ewell, and with that act he becomes a part of southern honor. He might have been a hero. Had a jury heard the case, his trial would have entertained the entire region. The community was unsettled from the rape trial, and this avenged death in the name of southern justice would have set well in Maycomb, Alabama. Boo Radley has been outside of southern honor, however, and he is a shy man. Lee has the sheriff explain the pitfalls of southern justice when he says, "Know what'd happen then? All the ladies in Maycomb includin' my wife'd be knocking on his door bringing angel food cakes. To my way of thinkin' . . . that's a sin. . . . If it was any other man it'd be different." The reader discovers that southern justice through the courts is not a blessing. It is a carnival.

Autobiographical Aspects of *To Kill a Mockingbird*

When Harper Lee was five years old the Scottsboro trial began. In one of the most celebrated southern trials, nine blacks were accused of raping two white girls. The first trial took place in Jackson County, Alabama. All nine were convicted. Monroeville, Lee's hometown, knew about the case. Retrials continued for six years, and with each new trial it became more obvious that southern justice for blacks was different from southern justice for whites. Harper Lee's father was a lawyer during that time. Her mother's maiden name was Finch. Harper Lee attended law school, a career possibility suggested to Scout by well-meaning adults in the novel. *To Kill a Mockingbird* is set in 1935, midpoint for the Scottsboro case.

Scout Finch faces the realities of southern society within the same age span that Harper Lee faced Scottsboro. The timeline is also the same. Although Lee's father was not the Scottsboro lawyer who handled that trial, he was a southern man of honor related to the famous gentleman soldier, Robert E. Lee. It is likely that Harper Lee's father was the author's model for Atticus Finch and that the things Atticus told Scout were the kinds of things Ama Lee told his daughter. The attitudes depicted are ones Harper Lee grew up with, both in terms of family pride and small town prejudices.

Literature Should Have Life Within the World

The censors' reactions to *To Kill a Mockingbird* were reactions to issues of race and justice. Their moves to ban the book derive from their own perspectives of the book's theme. Their "reader's response" criticism, usually based on one reading of the book, was personal and political. They needed to ban the book because it told them something about American society that they did not want to hear. That is precisely the problem facing any author of realistic fiction. Once the story becomes real, it can become grim. An author will use first-person flashback in story in order to let the reader live in another time, another place. Usually the storyteller is returning for a second view of the scene. The teller has experienced the events before and the story is being retold because the scene has left the storyteller uneasy. As the storyteller recalls the past both the listener and the teller see events in a new light. Both are working through troubled times in search of meaning. In the case of *To Kill a Mockingbird* the first-person retelling is not pleasant, but the underlying significance is with the narrative. The youthful personalities who are recalled are hopeful. Scout tells us of a time past when white people would lynch or convict a man because of the color of his skin. She also shows us three children who refuse to believe that the system is right, and she leaves us with the thought that most people will be nice if seen for what they are: humans with frailties. When discussing literary criticism, Theo D'Haen suggested that the good literary work should have a life within the world and be "part of the ongoing activities of that world." *To Kill a Mockingbird* continues to have life within the world; its ongoing activities in the realm of censorship show that it is a book which deals with regional moralism. The children in the story seem very human; they worry about their own identification, they defy parental rules, and they cry over injustices. They mature in Harper Lee's novel, and they lose their innocence. So does the reader. If the readers are young, they may believe Scout when she says, "nothin's real scary except in books." If the readers are older they will have learned that life is as scary, and they will be prepared to meet some of its realities.

Atticus Finch—Right and Wrong

Monroe H. Freedman

Monroe H. Freedman is a professor of law at Hofstra Law School. He is the recipient of numerous awards, including the Martin Luther King Award, for "decades of work to advance human dignity and social justice."

Atticus Finch has been deemed a hero of justice, a mythological paragon of social activism. But although Atticus admirably defended Tom Robinson, he was no antiracism activist. First, Atticus did not volunteer *to defend Tom Robinson; he was given a court order to do so. Then there is Atticus's complacence to racism, clearly portrayed in his confession (regarding defending Tom): "I'd hoped to get through life without a case of this kind. . . ."*

This is not to dismiss Atticus's fine attributes: He's a good father, treats all (black and white) with respect, and practices patient humility. While these characteristics make him a fine human being, they do not add up to social justice hero.

Leo Frank was murdered by a lynch mob in Marietta, Georgia, on August 15, 1915. He had been found guilty of the murder of Mary Phagan, a thirteen-year-old girl who worked in his factory, but his sentence of death had been commuted to life imprisonment by Governor John M. Slaton, who believed him to be innocent. Frank was unquestionably denied due process at his trial and was almost certainly innocent. But what is material here is the anti-Semitism that poisoned the trial and that fired up the mob that murdered him.

Monroe H. Freedman, "Atticus Finch—Right and Wrong," *Alabama Law Review*, vol. 45, 1993–1994, p. 473. Copyright © 1993–1994 The University of Alabama School of Law. Reproduced by permission.

During the trial, crowds inside the courthouse chanted, "Hang the Jew." The judge and the defense attorneys were threatened that they would not leave the courtroom alive if the "damned Jew" were acquitted. There is reason to believe that jurors were subjected to similar intimidation. Witnesses swore in affidavits after the conviction that two jurors had made anti-Semitic remarks before the trial, including, "I am glad they indicted the God damn Jew. They ought to take him out and lynch him. And if I get on that jury I'd hang that Jew sure." The prosecutor told the jury about Jewish criminals, including "Schwartz, who killed a little girl in New York." The prosecutor also compared Frank to Judas Iscariot [according to the New Testament, an apostle of Jesus who betrayed him].

The members of the mob that lynched Leo Frank were among the "best citizens" of Marietta. They included a minister, two former appellate court justices, and a former sheriff. The Dean of the Atlanta Theological Seminary later described the lynchers as a select group, "sober, intelligent, of established good name and character—good American citizens" and led by a man who "bore 'as reputable [a] name as you would ever hear in a lawful community . . . a man honored and respected.'"

Other good citizens, who later took snapshots of Frank's body as it hung from an oak tree, "milled about happily, as if at a holiday barbecue." *The Marietta Journal and Courier* commented: "We are proud, indeed, to say that the body hanged for more than two hours amid a vast throng and no violence was done. Cobb county people are civilized. They are not barbarians."

But Leo Frank's lynching was not the end; it was the beginning. The men who hanged Frank had been part of a group who called themselves the Knights of Mary Phagan. After murdering Frank, this group provided the nucleus for the revival of the Ku Klux Klan in an elaborate ritual on a mountain top just outside of Atlanta.

Walking in Another's Skin

Some twenty years and hundreds of lynchings later, a gang of Klansmen, in sheets and hoods, bearing crosses and torches, gathered at the home of Sam Levy [the Jewish owner of the general store in *To Kill a Mockingbird*] and his family in Atticus Finch's Maycomb, Alabama. The Levys would have known what had happened to Leo Frank, and of the Klan's record of terrorism in the following years. They would also have known that the Klan had formed alliances with American Nazis during the 1930s. Let's take the advice of Atticus Finch, then, and do something that he failed to do. Let's climb into the skin of Sam Levy and his wife and his children, and walk around in it.

The Levys are alone against the hooded mob. Atticus Finch is not there for them, nor are any of the other good people of Maycomb. Recall how Tom Robinson is unable to sleep and cringes, full of dread, behind the wall of his cell in Maycomb's jail when the Maycomb lynch mob comes for him. In the same way, Mrs. Levy and her children would be wide awake, cowering in terror behind the wall of their home, fearing that their husband and father would be shot by the mob, or that he would be carried away and later found hung, another piece of strange fruit swinging from the branch of a Southern tree. They also would know that Klan torches are used to burn down houses with people in them. The children would be crying, muffling their sobs so that the mob could not hear them.

And Sam Levy—with his wife's and children's lives and his own life in jeopardy—Levy would know that his only chance, and a slim one, would be to try to face down the mob alone. So he stands on his porch, stomach churning, heart pounding, "and [tells] 'em things had come to a pretty pass, he'd sold 'em the very sheets on their backs." His courageous bluff works. "Sam made 'em so ashamed of themselves they went away," Finch complacently recounted.

Atticus's Half-Truths

And what of Finch's judgment on the Levys' night of terror, and the lasting trauma to the Jewish parents and to their children? The Klan, he says, "couldn't find anybody to scare." The Klan, in fact, wasn't in the business of scaring—much less harming—anyone. "Way back about nineteen-twenty there was a Klan, but it was a political organization more than anything." Nineteen-twenty, recall, was three years after the lynching of Leo Frank. And, "[n]o, we don't have mobs and that nonsense in Maycomb. I've never heard of a gang in Maycomb." When Jem replies, "Ku Klux got after some Catholics one time," Finch does not explain that Catholics were the frequent victims of Klan violence. Instead he responds evasively: "Never heard of any Catholics in Maycomb either. . . . [Y]ou're confusing that with something else."

Is this just a father trying to quiet his children's fears with falsehoods and evasions? Not if we are to believe Finch himself: "Jack! When a child asks you something, answer him, for goodness' sake. But don't make a production of it. Children are children, but they can spot an evasion quicker than adults, and evasion simply muddles 'em." "I just hope that Jem and Scout come to me for their answers instead of listening to the town," he adds.

And those who extol Finch as a paragon of moral character, praise him most for his truthfulness, especially to his children. [According to Timothy Hall] "[T]ruthfulness was stamped upon his character like an Indian head on an old nickel. . . ."

Consider, then, the moral truth that he tells to the children when they experience the lynch mob outside the jail. Walter Cunningham, a leader of the mob, is "basically a good man," he teaches them, "he just has his blind spots along with the rest of us." It just happens that Cunningham's blind spot (along with the rest of us?) is a homicidal hatred of black people. And when Jem replies, with the innocent wisdom of a child, that attempted murder is not just a "blind spot," Finch condescendingly explains to him: "[S]on, you'll understand folks a little better when you're older. A mob's always made up of people, no matter what. Mr. Cunningham was part of a mob last night, but he was still a man."

Atticus's Presentism

What are we to make of this fatuousness [unconscious foolishness]? That a lynch mob is not a lynch mob because it's "made up of people"? That because Cunningham is "still a man," he has no moral responsibility for attempted murder? Who does have moral (and legal) responsibility for a wrongful action if not the person who commits the wrong?

One of the charges I have faced for past criticisms of Atticus Finch is "presentism." This clumsy neologism [a word created to apply new concepts] is meant to express the idea that it is unfair to hold someone in an earlier time to moral standards that we recognize today. Lest anyone miss the point, this contention is derived from cultural relativism. This is a philosophy that rejects the idea that there are any moral values that are absolute (or, at least, prima facie [by first instance]) and eternal. Instead, morality is equated with the notions of right and wrong that are recognized in the culture of a particular time and place. Slavery? Apartheid? Lynching? Sacrificing babies? Well, the cultural relativist says, we might not approve, but who are we to judge the moral standards of people in another time or place?

Prima Facie Principles of Right and Wrong

So let me declare myself. I do believe that there are prima facie principles of right and wrong (which can be called Natural Law), which each of us is capable of recognizing by the use of experience, intellect, and conscience. There may not be many such principles of right and wrong, but the terrorizing of the Levy family, the attempted lynching of Tom Robinson, and the apartheid that Atticus Finch practiced every day of his life—those things are wrong today, and they were wrong in Maycomb, Alabama, in the 1930s.

Again, let's take Finch's advice. Let's get inside the skin of the black people of Maycomb and walk around in an ordinary day of their lives. They endure, and their children grow up experiencing minute-by-minute reminders of separateness premised upon their innate inferiority. They are compelled to live in a ghetto near the town garbage dump. They cannot use the white only rest rooms, the white only water fountains, the white only lunch counters, or the white only parks. If their children go to school, their segregated schools, like their churches, have few if any books. They are even segregated in the courtroom in which Finch practices law. The jobs allowed to them are the most menial. And they face the everyday threat of lawless but condoned violence for any real or imagined stepping out of line.

Tom Robinson knows this, and he knows that it will cost him his life. The last thing he says to Atticus before they take him to the prison camp is: "Good-bye, Mr. Finch, there ain't nothin' you can do now, so there ain't no use tryin.'" That day, "he just gave up hope." And, of course, Tom Robinson is right. He is shot to death—with seventeen bullets—on the claim that a gentle man with a useless arm, in a prison yard the size of a football field, in plain view of guards with guns, broke into a blind, raving charge in a hopeless attempt to climb over the fence and escape.

You can believe this improbable story, as Finch purports to do. But I believe (and Harper Lee appears to believe) that Tom Robinson was goaded into a desperate, futile run for the fence on the threat of being shot where he stood. Underwood's editorial in the *Maycomb Tribune* calls it a "senseless" killing—not what one would call a killing, with fair warning, of a raving man about to surmount a prison fence and escape. And if Finch averts his eyes from the truth, Scout faces it straight on.

"Tom was a dead man," she realizes, "the minute Mayella Ewell opened her mouth and screamed."

Atticus's Complacence

Throughout his relatively comfortable and pleasant life in Maycomb, Atticus Finch knows about the grinding, ever-present humiliation and degradation of the black people of Maycomb; he tolerates it; and sometimes he even trivializes and condones it. Nor does Finch need the presentism of a Northern liberal six decades later to tell him that these things are wrong. He himself accurately diagnoses "Maycomb's usual disease . . . reasonable people go[ing] stark raving mad when anything involving a Negro comes up." "[I]t's all adding up," he recognizes, "and one of these days we're going to pay the bill for it." But he hopes that the struggle for justice won't come during his children's lifetimes. For Finch, the civil rights movement of the 1960s is inevitable, but decades too soon.

The charge of presentism fails also when we consider that other whites of the time—born, raised, and living in Finch's South—are able to see that the oppression of blacks is morally wrong. Dill, nine years old, runs out of Robinson's trial, physically sickened by the prosecutor's racist baiting of Robinson. "It ain't right, somehow it ain't right to do 'em that way. Hasn't anybody got any business talkin' like that—it just makes me sick."

Maudie Atkinson is another who recognizes the injustice against blacks and, she tells the children, they'd be surprised how many others think the same way. They include prominent and respected members of the community: Judge John Taylor and Sheriff Heck Tate, the landowner Link Deas, and the editor Braxton Underwood. They include Dolphus Raymond: "Cry about the simple hell people give other people—without even thinking. Cry about the hell white people give colored folks, without even stopping to think that they're people, too." And Jem, in response to Finch's explanation about the "ugly facts of life" and of Southern justice, also recognizes right and wrong. "Doesn't make it right," he says, beating his fist softly on his knee.

No Paragon of Social Activism

What, then, do I expect of Atticus *as a lawyer*? First, because there has been some misunderstanding in the past, let's be clear about what I don't expect. I have never suggested that Finch should have dedicated his life to [according to Timothy Hall] "working on the front lines for the N.A.A.C.P." On the contrary, in rejecting the notion that Atticus Finch is a role model for today's lawyers, here is what I said: "Don't misunderstand. I'm not saying that I would present as role models those truly admirable lawyers who, at great personal sacrifice, have dedicated their entire professional lives to fighting for social justice. That's too easy to preach and too hard to practice."

In fact, part of the point of my commentary is that Finch's adulators [admirers] inaccurately represent him as a paragon of social activism. . . . Also, it is Finch's adulators who insist upon rewriting the book to create a mythologized hero. Typical is a recent piece stating that Finch "decides" to represent an indigent. . . . defendant [impoverished]. This is wrong on two counts. First, Finch does not choose to represent Tom Robinson. He accepts a court appointment, but candidly says, "You know, I'd hoped to get through life without a case of this kind, but John Taylor pointed at me and said, 'You're It.'"

Second, it is inaccurate to say that Finch's friends subject him to obloquy [disgrace]. It is true that many of the townpeople do, but not Finch's friends, not the people whose opinions he values. In fact, those people admire Finch for taking the case and for giving Robinson zealous representation.

Maudie Atkinson is one. She gives Finch the highest praise she can. "We're so rarely called on to be Christians," she tells Jem, "but when we are, we've got men like Atticus to go for us." And when Jem says, "Wish the rest of the county thought that," she replies, "You'd be surprised how many of us do." In addition to Maudie Atkinson, these include the most prominent people in Maycomb—Judge John Taylor, Sheriff Heck Tate, property owner Link Deas, and newspaper editor Braxton Underwood—"people like us."

Redeeming "Liberty and Justice for All"

I don't say this to disparage Finch, but for the sake of accuracy regarding presentism. Disparagement comes with my next point, which considers what it means that Finch "hoped to get through life without a case of this kind." It means that Atticus Finch never in his professional life voluntarily takes a pro bono case in an effort to ameliorate the evil—which he himself and others recognize—in the apartheid of Maycomb, Alabama. Forget about "working on the front lines for the NAACP." Here is a man who does not voluntarily use his legal training and skills—not once, ever—to make the slightest change in the pervasive social injustice of his own town.

Atticus Finch is, after all, a skilled lawyer, a friend of the rich and powerful, and for many years a member of the state legislature. As a legislator, in fact, his diligence in reorganizing the tax system keeps him from his family and is a matter for respectful editorial comment in the newspapers. Could he not introduce one bill to mitigate the evils of segregation? Could he not work with Judge Taylor in an effort to desegregate the courthouse? Could he not take, voluntarily, a single appeal in a death penalty case? And could he not represent a Tom Robinson just once without a court order to do so? As Finch acknowledges, Robinson's case is not unique. Referring to the jury's conviction of an innocent black man, he says, "They've done it before . . . and they'll do it again."

But let's assume, for the sake of discussion, that I Am guilty of presentism. Assume too that anything Finch tried to do would be futile (which is a familiar justification for being a bystander to evil). Even if those contentions have merit, does that make Finch a role model for today's lawyer? As former ABA [American Bar Association] president Talbot D'Alemberte has pointed out, eighty percent of the legal needs of the poor are today going unmet. Carrying out a court appointment, as Finch did, will comply with the lawyer's oath "in a technical sense," D'Alemberte reminds us, but unless more lawyers *volunteer* their services, we will not redeem our country's and our profession's pledge of "liberty and justice for all."

Atticus: Human, Not Myth

But in saying that Finch is not an adequate role model for today's lawyer, I want to avoid the over-simplification of his adulators. Finch has an enviable array of admirable qualities and, in one instance, he is truly courageous.

He is a loving, patient, and understanding father, successfully coping with the burden of being a single parent. In his personal relations with other people, black and white, he unfailingly treats everyone with respect. Professionally, he is a superb advocate, a wise counsellor, and a conscientious legislator. A crack shot, he never touches a gun, except to protect the community from a rabid dog. Even when he heroically waits for and faces down the lynch mob, he arms himself only with a newspaper.

In short, Atticus Finch is both more and less than the mythical figure that has been made of him. He is human—sometimes right and sometimes wrong. And one criticizes Atticus Finch not from a position of superiority, but with respect, like a sports columnist reporting the imperfection in an athlete whose prowess he himself could never match.

Representation of Race and Justice in *To Kill a Mockingbird*

Joseph Crespino

Joseph Crespino is a professor of history at Emory University. In 2007, he published In Search of Another Country: Mississippi and the Conservative Counterrevolution.

To Kill a Mockingbird *is possibly the most frequently read book concerning race in America. Since publication, readers have praised Atticus Finch's "racial heroism"; as a white middle-class man who wholeheartedly defended a black man in the courtroom of the Jim Crow South, Atticus has long been linked with justice and humanity. Yet recent objections against Atticus's tolerance of his society's bigotry and hatred question whether he did enough in the fight against racism to deserve the status of "racial hero." Many challenge this critical perception of Atticus, stating that he was limited by the historical moment in which he lived. Because of this, he shouldn't be judged by our modern standards of racial heroism, but rather placed within the context of his time.*

One of the basic questions raised in the 1960s that reverberates in multiculturalism today is who in our society is allowed to speak authoritatively on racial issues. Over the course of the twentieth century, but particularly with the flowering of African American studies, the era in which white intellectuals debated the "Negro problem" among themselves has ended once and for all. In countless cultural productions and scholarly works from the civil rights era and more recent decades, African Americans are the subjects in the exploration

Joseph Crespino, "The Strange Career of Atticus Finch," *Southern Cultures*, vol. 6, summer 2000, pp. 9–29. Reproduced by permission.

of racial inequality in American history and life. And yet looming among the most popular and enduring works on racial matters since the 1960s is Harper Lee's *To Kill a Mockingbird*, the Depression-era account of Atticus Finch's legal defense of a black man wrongly accused of raping a white woman, told through the eyes of Finch's nine-year-old daughter, Scout.

America's Struggle for Racial Equality

In the twentieth century, *To Kill a Mockingbird* is probably the most widely read book dealing with race in America, and its protagonist, Atticus Finch, the most enduring fictional image of racial heroism. Published in the fall of 1960, the novel had already sold five hundred thousand copies and been translated into ten languages by the time it received the Pulitzer Prize in 1961. The story was almost immediately snatched up by Hollywood, and the Alan Pakula-directed film had the double distinction of landing Gregory Peck an Oscar for his portrayal of Finch and giving Robert Duvall, with a brief role as the mysterious Boo Radley, the first of his seemingly countless screen appearances. It is estimated that by 1982 *To Kill a Mockingbird* had sold over fifteen million copies, and a 1991 American "Survey of Lifetime Reading Habits" by the Book-of-the-Month Club and the Library of Congress revealed that next to the Bible the book was "most often cited in making a difference" in people's lives.

The novel influenced a generation of Americans raised during the turbulent years of the 1960s and 1970s. Former Clinton adviser James Carville, who spent his formative years in the 1960s South, reflected on Harper Lee's achievement: "I just knew, the minute I read it, that she was right and I had been wrong. I don't want to make it noble, or anything. I was just bored with all the talk of race." . . .

Given [its] legacy, the dearth of critical commentary on the novel is surprising. Literary critic Eric Sundquist writes,

"It is something of a mystery that the book has failed to arouse the antagonism now often prompted by another great novelistic depiction of the South . . . *Adventures of Huckleberry Finn*, which arguably uses the word nigger with more conscious irony than does *To Kill a Mockingbird* and whose antebellum [the period just before the war most often refers to the Civil War] framework and moral complexity ought to be a far greater bulwark against revisionist denunciation." A critique as basic as noting Atticus Finch's paternalism did not emerge until recently, and even then such a reading has been contested by Finch defenders.

The enduring career of *To Kill a Mockingbird* as a story of racial justice, and of Atticus Finch as a racial hero, reveals much about American racial politics in the second half of the twentieth century. From 1960s liberalism to 1990s multiculturalism, from the inchoate [early] conservatism of [five-term Republican senator Barry] Goldwater through that of the Reagan-Bush era, Atticus Finch has been both admired and scorned by liberals and conservatives alike. Tracing Atticus's place within the American imagination reveals some of the major fault lines in the struggle for racial equality over the past forty years and allows us to look again at how competing groups have flamed racial issues in America. . . .

Lee's Narrative Strategies

Lee's characters and choice of narrative strategies in *To Kill a Mockingbird* reflect the moral tensions that all liberals faced in the Jim Crow South. They combine the passion and ambivalence characteristic of southerners drawn to the South's agrarian [rural] tradition and heritage but frustrated by the South's ugly racial history. Lee places Atticus Finch within the tradition of southern progressivism by linking him with the turn-of-the-century New South booster Henry Grady [19th century editor for the *Atlanta Constitution* who promoted a new, economically vibrant, South]. Atticus advises Jem to read the speeches of Grady, who, if not a believer in the absolute equality of the races, was enough of a racial progressive to be despised by many white southerners of his day. . . .

Atticus's liberal pedigree comes through most clearly in his concern for his children. In a conversation with his brother, Atticus worries about the effect Tom Robinson's trial and Maycomb's racism will have on Jem and Scout. "You know what's going to happen as well as I do, Jack, and I hope and pray I can get Jem and Scout through it without bitterness, and most of all, without catching Maycomb's usual disease. Why reasonable people go stark raving mad when anything involving a Negro comes up, is something I don't pretend to understand. . . . I just hope that Jem and Scout come to me for their answers instead of listening to the town. I hope they trust me enough." Atticus's puzzling over why people go "mad" and his concern with "Maycomb's usual disease" foreshadows the following scene in which Jem and Scout watch from the porch as their father shoots and kills a mad dog running loose on the street in front of the Finch home. The dog seems a likely symbol of white racism in the South. Up to this point, Scout and Jim think of their father as "feeble" because he was "nearly fifty" and did not play in the church football games. By shooting the dog, Atticus confirms his virility [manliness] both as a father protecting his children and as a southern liberal dealing with white racism.

It is significant that Calpurnia, the Finch's domestic servant and the lone African American in the scene, is the one who alerts Atticus to the dog's presence and warns the all-white neighborhood to stay off the streets. In Calpurnia, Lee recognizes the role African Americans played in exposing white racism; through her Lee acknowledges the working-class African American civil rights protesters in the South who revealed the ugly face of Jim Crow to liberal America. While Lee does not entirely deny African Americans a place in the destruction of southern racism, in this scene their role is limited to that of warning the liberal white hero of the danger to come. As Finch bravely stops the mad dog in his tracks, Calpurnia watches on the porch with the children. It is also significant that Heck Tate, the Maycomb County sheriff, arrives with Atticus to stop the dog. Finch expects Sheriff Tate to shoot the dog, but the sheriff hesitates and then anxiously hands the gun to Finch: "For God's sake, Mr. Finch, look where he is! . . . I can't shoot that well and you know it!" Atticus, a crack shot as everyone in town but his children knows, finishes the responsibility. The figure of Heck Tate in this scene may well refer to the elected officials of the South, such as Arkansas governor Orval Faubus in Little Rock, who through fear, incompetence, or narrow-mindedness were unable to face down the mad dog of southern racism. Only Atticus possesses the skill and courage to put the rabid dog to rest.

Regional Problems of the South

Lee's vision of liberal racial change remained distinctly regional; Atticus Finch is not a wild-eyed reformer who rejects his southern heritage. Lee believed that racial change would come through liberalism refined by a certain understanding of how the world works—particularly how white southerners work when it comes to the explosive issue of race. When Jem, frustrated by Tom Robinson's conviction, suggests doing away with all juries, Atticus stops him. "Those are twelve reasonable men in everyday life, Tom's jury, but you saw something come between them and reason," Atticus tells Jem. "The one place where a man ought to get a square deal is in a courtroom, be he any color of the rainbow, but people have a way of carrying their resentments right into a jury box." Atticus understands that America's historic claim to justice and equality could not be realized without racial justice in the South, but he recognizes as well the extreme difficulties involved, given the prejudices of his region.

Similarly, Scout's precocious literacy becomes a symbol of southern liberals' competence in dealing with racism. At Scout's first day of school she encounters a recent college graduate schooled in what Jem mistakenly calls "the Dewey Decimal system," Lee's reference it seems to pedagogical techniques developed by the northern, progressive educator John Dewey. In the first half of the twentieth century, Dewey had become one of the most prominent liberal members of the American academy. Lee's indirect reference to him here encapsulates her vision of the relationship between northern and southern liberalism. Scout does not need the new, "improved" pedagogical techniques of the young teacher; she knows how to read already. She was taught by her father, Atticus, the model of southern erudition [knowledge that is gained through study and reading]. Scout's literacy here is a symbol of the South's ability to analyze its own problems, to deal with them in its own regionally specific way.

Atticus's Heroic Qualities

Part of Atticus Finch's heroic power lies in his ability to embrace the need and the moral imperative for racial change without rejecting his native South. He reminds Scout that though this time they were not fighting against "the Yankees, we're fighting our friends," she should hold no grudges because "no matter how bitter things get, they're still our friends and this is still our home." But in this scene Lee comforts white southerners fearful of the change that was imminent in the South. As Eric Sundquist writes [in "Blues for Atticus Finch"], "Just as the South closed ranks against the nation at the outset of desegregation . . . so *To Kill a Mockingbird* carefully narrows the terms on which changed race relations are going to be brought about in the South." Through Atticus Finch, Lee reassured anxious white southerners that civil rights change could come to the South peacefully, without bitterness, and without dividing the white southern community. After all, the southern liberals leading the change were longtime friends and neighbors; they were, first and [a former Mississippi governor and U.S. senator known for his white-supremist beliefs] foremost, southerners.

At the same time, for readers North and South who admired the book's racial mores, Atticus represented the continuity of American values of justice and equality. The novel tells us that even in the Depression-era Jim Crow South, the era of Scottsboro [trials of nine black youths accused of raping two white women in the 1930s] and [Theodore G.] Bilbo, there existed within the South men like Atticus Finch who would be the seeds of the transformation to come. Atticus is a modern hero who, while embodying the most noble aspects of the southern tradition, also transcended the limits of that tradition and attained a liberal, morally rational racial viewpoint that was seen as quintessentially American.

Above all, Atticus's morality drives the novel, a morality that is as evident in *To Kill a Mockingbird* as it is in one of American liberalism's signature documents, the Supreme Court's majority decision in *Brown v. Board of Education* (1954). [Chief Justice] Earl Warren's decision [to desegregate public schools] resonated with moral authority: "Such considerations apply with added force to children in grade and high schools. To separate them from others of similar age and qualifications solely because of their race generates a feeling of inferiority as to their status in the community that may affect their hearts and minds in a way unlikely ever to be undone." In *To Kill a Mockingbird* Lee's decision to report Atticus's heroics through the perspective of his nine-year-old daughter is crucial in reinforcing the moral impulse that it is children who ultimately have the most at risk in the nation's struggle to end racial segregation. The project was to be carried out by good liberals like Atticus, but even then it was most effective because it was backed by the moral weight of a child's voice. This is the meaning of one of the novel's most famous scenes, in which Scout faces down a lynch mob that is ready to lynch Tom Robinson. As Sundquist writes, scenes such as this "are calculated to substantiate the ethical authority driving *Brown.*" . . .

Maycomb's People

Atticus's elite class position within the small southern town of Maycomb is an essential part of his heroism. Atticus is a paternal figure not only for blacks but poor whites as well. In a telling passage, Jem explains to his sister Maycomb's four different classes: "There's four kinds of folks in the world. There's the ordinary kind like us and the neighbors, there's the kind like the Cunninghams out in the woods, the kind like the Ewells down at the dump, and the Negroes." While Scout denies these distinctions, she lives in a world clearly divided along class lines. Atticus explains to Jem, "You and Jean Louise . . . are not from run-of-the-mill people . . . you are the product of several generations' gentle breeding . . . and you should try to live up to your name." Though they are both members of the white working class, the novel distinguishes between the Cunninghams and the Ewells based on the degree to which they aspire to bourgeois values—the degree to which they accommodate themselves to the hegemony [the predominant influence over others] of the dominant class. The young Walter Cunningham goes hungry rather than borrow money from the teacher that he knows he cannot pay back. Mr. Cunningham diligently pays back his legal debt to Atticus Finch through subsistence crops from his farm. Although Mr. Cunningham is a member of Tom Robinson's potential lynch mob, he politely retreats when faced by Scout's authentic moral presence. In contrast, the Ewells place no value on education, showing up the first day and never coming to school again. Mr. Ewell breaks the law by hunting out of season, and Mayella Ewell breaks the fundamental code of middle-class southern womanhood by desiring the black body of Tom Robinson.

In the context of Black Power politics, one of the book's peripheral characters—Lula, the black-separatist member of Calpurnia's church—becomes one of its most interesting. Lula challenges Calpurnia for bringing the Finch children to worship at the black church: "You ain't got no business bringin' white chillun here—they got their church, we got our'n. It is our church, ain't it, Miss Cal?" Lula reminds Calpurnia that she is a servant to the Finches, not an equal: "Yeah, an' I reckon you's company at the Finch house durin' the week." Calpurnia verbally spars with Lula in front of the church, reverting to an African American dialect that the children had never heard from her before. Lula mysteriously disappears from the scene, and the rest of the church comforts the children, telling them they should ignore Lula: "She's a troublemaker from way back, got fancy ideas an' haughty ways— we're mighty glad to have you all." Lee uses this scene to reveal her expectations for what the proper African American response to the white presence should be. Lula objects to both the white children's freedom to enter the black world and the inordinate respect they receive once they are there. Lula's position in relation to Calpurnia reproduces Black Power's position toward African American liberals during the civil rights era. Lee removes all doubt as to which model white America prefers. . . .

Debating Atticus

Although *To Kill a Mockingbird* has maintained its popularity as a modern-day race tale, in the aftermath of Black Power and with conservative ascendancy, both liberals and conservatives have become markedly more ambivalent in their views of Atticus Finch as an American racial hero. Certain school districts across the country have censored the novel for its sexual content, and more recently some have banned it because of its depiction of societal racism. *To Kill a Mockingbird* has increasingly become a battleground where cultural critics from the left and right debate their respective views of contemporary racial politics. For example, a 1992 debate among legal scholars amounted to a public trial of Atticus Finch. Monroe Freedman, a law professor at Hofstra University, wrote an article in *Legal Times* titled "Atticus Finch, Esq., R.I.P." that questioned Finch's role as a model of humanity and morality for the legal profession. Freedman argued that as a state legislator and community leader in a segregated society, Finch was the "passive participant in that pervasive injustice." Freedman would extend his comments later in a symposium at the University of Alabama: "Throughout his relatively comfortable and pleasant life in Maycomb, Atticus Finch knows about the grinding, ever-present humiliation and degradation of the black people of Maycomb; he tolerates it; and sometimes he even trivializes and condones it." Freedman de-emphasizes the personal heroism of Finch to focus on the larger structural racism of which he was a part and which, in Freedman's estimation, he did little to combat.

Freedman's critique appalled many of his colleagues. . . . In his eagerness to challenge notions of legal ethics, Freedman does ignore Finch's more commendable character traits, but the public outcry against his article suggests that something more was involved.

Many who objected argued that Freedman ignored Finch's individual act of racial heroism and its power to inspire similar acts today. In an article revealingly titled "Atticus Finch *De Novo*: In Defense of Gentlemen," Timothy J. Dunn charged that Freedman underestimated "the value to the human spirit of acts of heroic value." No less an authority than the president of the American Bar Association, Talbot D'Alemberte, rose in defense of Finch. "Sixty years after Judge Taylor appointed Atticus Finch to defend a poor black man in *To Kill a Mockingbird*, these . . . fictional heroes still inspire us," wrote

D'Alemberte. "Finch rose above racism and injustice to defend the principle that all men and women deserve their day in court."

Dunn and D'Alemberte defended Atticus Finch not just as a man ahead of his times, but as a model of decorum in the very sensitive arena of race relations. Yet their defense did not take into account the many differences between Atticus's era and the present. As Freedman pointed out, Atticus Finch acted heroically in 1930s segregated Alabama, but to a modern reader the limits of his heroism should be fairly evident. Racism today does not always rear its head in such blatant and perverse forms as it did in Depression-era Alabama. . . .

Deconstructing Atticus

[There] is [a] strangeness [regarding] Atticus Finch's career: once a tool of liberal racial politics, Atticus has now become the pawn of racial conservatism. The right, in its insistence on focusing on racial bias on the personal level, glorifies Atticus Finch–style racial heroism. If racism exists only on an individual basis, then racial reform can occur only through individual moral reform—not through social or structural change that might challenge the legal, economic, or political status quo. As conservatives beatify the racial heroism of Atticus Finch, they fight the symptoms of the disease and fail to look for a cure that might get at the issue of white privilege.

How is it in a multicultural America that Atticus Finch and his various cinematic progeny [descendants] continue to be held up as racial heroes? One explanation is that having a white racial hero at the center of the story allows the public to conceptualize race issues within an individual, moralistic framework. Movies traffic in stereotypes: racist rednecks, innocent black victims, white liberal heroes. Unfortunately, so do American politicians. White people solving the "American Dilemma" was the fundamental assumption of postwar racial liberalism; today application of the same principle underlies claims of reverse racism and forms the basis for conservative opposition to affirmative action and declarations of "the end of racism." Ultimately, it is the belief that even though racism exists it cannot last because it is an aberration from American ideals of equality. Freedman's critique highlighted the structural racism of segregation-era Alabama but failed to link Finch to the obfuscation [puzzlement] of white privilege that persists in America today. It should come as no surprise that when we place Atticus Finch under the lens of contemporary multicultural politics, we see the same symptoms that Black Power initially diagnosed in the sickness of American liberalism—a paternalistic and hopelessly moderated view of social change. . . .

The question of where Atticus Finch fits into this movement remains. My initial reaction is that the American social commentators who still invoke Atticus Finch's image, and the secondary school teachers who assign *To Kill a Mockingbird* in their classes year after year, should let Atticus come down from his perch as an emblem of American racial heroism. Harper Lee described her novel as "a simple love story"; while this element of the book cannot be separated from the novel's racial politics, one should not necessarily swim against the tide of Atticus's continuing popularity. This is a difficult thing to do because what one person sees as Finch's gentlemanly demeanor towards women another might characterize as sexist patronizing; what is decorum and self-restraint in racial matters to some may well seem small-minded and compromising to others.

My suggestion is that we reassign *To Kill a Mockingbird* from English class to history class and that rather than dismissing Atticus we deconstruct him. Certainly, we can no longer simply hold him up as a racial hero, for in a multicultural society that honors the dignity and agency of all people it is not clear what one would actually look like.

Racism and Other Injustice in Harper Lee's Writing

Laurie Champion

Laurie Champion is a professor of English at San Diego State University, Imperial Valley. She has published extensively in the field of literary criticism and theory.

Connotations of "right" and "left" occur throughout To Kill a Mockingbird. *Here, "right" is symbolic for "good," "just," or "tolerant," while references to "left" symbolize "bad," "unjust," or "racist." For instance, on the side of "right" fall Atticus Finch, who is nearly blind in his left eye; Tom Robinson, whose left hand is lame; and Jem Finch, who has an injured left arm. On the "left" side are Bob Ewell, who is left-handed; the rabid dog, whose right legs are weaker than its left; and Mayella Ewell, whose right eye is injured and left eye is left intact. Whether or not it was Harper Lee's intention, this "right" and "left" symbolism is prevalent in her novel.*

Throughout Harper Lee's *To Kill a Mockingbird*, besides the ordinary connotations of "right" and "left" as opposing spatial directions, the terms also work on a subtler level: "right" suggesting virtue and "left" suggesting iniquity.

Right and Left in the Trial Scenes

Connotations of "right" and "left" play a crucial role during the climactic trial scenes. Building evidence against Bob Ewell, Atticus asks Sheriff Tate which one of Mayella's eyes was bruised the night she was attacked, and Tate replies, "Her left."

Laurie Champion, "Lee's *To Kill a Mockingbird* (Racism in Harper Lee's Works)," *The Explicator*, vol. 61, summer 2003, pp. 234–236. Copyright © 2003 by Helen Dwight Reid Educational Foundation. Reproduced with permission of the Helen Dwight Reid Educational Foundation, published by Heldref Publications, 1319 18th Street, NW, Washington, DC 20036-1802.

Atticus asks, "Was it her left facing you or her left looking the same way you were?" Tate says, "Oh yes, that'd make it her right. It was her right eye, Mr. Finch. I remember now, she was bunged up on that side of her face." Bob says that he agrees with Tate's testimony that Mayella's "right eye was blackened." A reading of the transcript of Tate's testimony reminds the jury that Tate testified that Mayella's right eye was black: "[W]hich eye her left oh yes that'd make it her right it was her right eye. [. . .] [I]t was her right eye I said—." Directional words "right" and "left" are repeated, emphasizing the dichotomy [separation of contradictory things]. Literally, Mayella could not see clearly from her right eye when it was bruised; symbolically, Mayella cannot act morally.

Whereas Mayella's right eye is bruised, Atticus is nearly blind in his left eye, both literally and figuratively: "Whenever he wanted to see something well, he turned his head and looked from his right eye." Later, when Atticus scolds Scout, he pins her "to the wall with his good eye." When Atticus questions Mayella on the witness stand, he "turned his good right eye to the witness." Atticus uses his "right" eye, his "good" eye for wisdom. Both "good" and "right" express moral undertones, as in "the good," suggesting wisdom and insight are products of "good" eyes.

Portrayals of Mayella's bruised right eye also contrast portrayals of Tom's left arm, which was "fully twelve inches shorter than his right, and hung dead at his side." Tom's left arm "hung dead," just as immorality is dead in him. While the court observes Tom's mangled left arm, Atticus asks Mayella, "He blackened your left eye with his right fist?" Atticus's point is made, and with repeated use of various connotations of words such as "left," "right," and "side," implications of morality abound.

Atticus proves Bob is left-handed, providing circumstantial evidence that Bob attacked Mayella. Atticus says, "Mayella Ewell was beaten savagely by someone who led almost exclusively with his left." Bob signs a warrant "with his left hand," whereas Tom takes "the oath with the only good hand he possesses—his right hand". Bob is "led" by the immoral left, but Tom tells the truth, swearing with his "good" right hand. Tom's "good arm" parallels Atticus's "good eye," and in both cases "good" signifies proper function and virtue.

Before Tom's mangled left arm is exposed, Scout questions Tom's innocence. She says that if Mayella's "right eye was blacked and she was beaten mostly on the right side of the face, it would tend to show that a left-handed person did it. [. . .] But Tom Robinson could easily be left-handed, too. Like Mr. Heck Tate, I imagined a person facing me, went through a swift mental pantomime, and concluded that he might have held her with his right hand and pounded her with his left." Again, the words "right" and "left" are repeated. Scout also uses the word "facing," a directional word that represents the jury Tom faces and the truth the jury refuses to face.

Right-Left Dichotomy Throughout

Lee introduces a right-left dichotomy in the opening scene of *To Kill a Mockingbird*, a scene narrated many years after the events of the narrative proper. Scout says that Jem's "left arm was somewhat shorter than his right; when he stood or walked, the back of his hand was at right angles to his body . . ." Jem, like Tom, has an injured left arm and a healthy right arm. His hand turns at right angles, signifying his morally correct perspective. In the opening paragraph, Scout provides a framework for her story, disclosing that she will explain how Jem's accident occurred. As the plot unravels, readers are told how Jem hurt his arm. More important, readers come to understand Jem's moral development.

Immediately after Atticus shoots a rabid dog, Sheriff Tate runs to Atticus and taps "his finger on his forehead above his left eye." He says, "You were a little to the right, Mr. Finch." Atticus answers, "Always was . . ." Of course, Tate refers to the direction "right" as opposed to "center" or "left," but symbolically, Atticus looks to the "right," protects the neighborhood. The dog "walked erratically, as if his right legs were shorter than his left legs." The dog's lame right legs symbolize malevolence, his danger to society.

As in instances where "right" opposes "left," the term "right" designates that a specific spatial locale also has ethical undertones. Atticus tells Calpurnia that Tom stood "[r]ight in front of" the guards who shoot him. Tom stands both directly in front of the guards and on his own symbolic ethical ground. Inquiring if during the trial the children sat in the balcony of the courthouse, Miss Stephanie asks, "Wasn't it right close up there with all those—?" Symbolically, "right" refers to the truth, the section of the courthouse where people sit who support Tom, Atticus, and racial equity.

The term "left" also denotes what remains, what is "left" of something. Scout says that the dog "had made up what was left of his mind," turned around and began to walk toward the Finch's house. A few paragraphs later, Lee contrasts Atticus's mind with the dog's mind. After learning Atticus had once been called "Ol' One-Shot . . . the deadest shot in Maycomb County," Jem asks Miss Maudie why he never brags about his marksmanship talents. She answers, "People in their right minds never take pride in their talents." Here, the "right" mind literally refers to people who think straight, level-headed people—in this case, implying that Atticus is humble. Whereas the dog uses what is "left" of his mind to harm people, Atticus, in his "right" mind, exemplifies humility.

Atticus, Tom, and Jem represent moral virtue: Atticus uses his "right" mind and his "good, right" eye to defend Tom; Tom takes the oath with his "good, right" hand; and Jem, with his vigorous "right" arm, defends Tom. Contrarily, the rabid dog, Mayella, and Bob represent moral inequity. The dog's "left" legs are healthy; Mayella's "left" eye is healthy; and Bob is "left" handed. The rabid dog presents a physical threat to

Maycomb County, but Mayella and Bob present a social threat—the perpetuation of racism.

Atticus's virtue only enables him to eliminate the physical threat. That the jury convicts Tom in the end signals that Atticus loses his baffle against racism.

The False Accusation of Tom Robinson

Lisa Lindquist Dorr

Lisa Lindquist Dorr is an assistant professor of history at the University of Alabama. She has published many articles about the South.

In her novel, Harper Lee portrayed the "inevitability" of Tom Robinson's death once he, a black man, was accused of raping a white woman. As spoken by the novel's narrator, Scout: "Tom was a dead man the minute Mayella Ewell opened her mouth and screamed."

This inevitability may have rested solely on the shoulders of the poor white characters in the novel, as there was a long-strained relationship between blacks and poor whites. Many of the more "elite" whites in To Kill a Mockingbird, *including the judge, may not have concluded with "guilty," even as their own, more subtle, racism was present.*

In Harper Lee's 1960 novel, *To Kill a Mockingbird*, Tom Robinson, a crippled black man, is accused in 1935 of trying to rape a poor white woman in Maycomb, Alabama. Narrated by Scout Finch, a nine-year-old white girl and the daughter of Robinson's attorney, Atticus Finch, the trial reveals that rather than attempting to rape Mayella Ewell, Robinson is the victim of her sexual advances. When Mayella's father interrupted her seduction of Tom Robinson, he beat her and forced her to accuse Robinson of rape. Scout, realizing for the first time the ugly nature of race relations in the segregated South, informs the reader that Robinson's death is foreordained. "Atticus had

Lisa Lindquist Dorr, "Black-on-White Rape and Retribution in Twentieth-Century Virginia: Men, Even Negroes, Must Have Some Protection," *The Journal of Southern History*, vol. 66, November 2000, pp. 711–713, 715–716. Copyright © 2000 The Southern Historical Association. Reproduced by permission.

used every tool available to free men to save Tom Robinson, but in the secret courts of men's hearts Atticus had no case. Tom was a dead man the minute Mayella Ewell opened her mouth and screamed."

How Inevitable Was Tom Robinson's Death?

Robinson's fictional experience parallels the experiences of many black men in the twentieth-century South, and Scout echoes many scholars' conclusions when she claims that his death was inescapable. For historians, this sense of inevitability is so pervasive that it has shaped most analyses, not only of interracial sexual relations and lynching but also of race relations in the twentieth-century South. The words of Leon F. Litwack in 1998 recall those of Scout Finch: "For a black man, a sexual advance to a white woman was a certain invitation to a tortured death."

Robinson's death may not have been as inevitable as Scout believed. Lee makes clear that the whites in Maycomb were divided along class lines about Tom Robinson's guilt. The rural farmers who composed the jury refused to consider Atticus Finch's appeals to rationality, and they found Robinson guilty. After the jurors had rendered their verdict, their role in the case was finished. The verdict was a catharsis—a performance that resolved the racial tensions raised by Mayella Ewell's accusation. However, white legal authorities, whose class interests were not always aligned with those of the white jurors, controlled the disposition of Tom Robinson's sentence. Elite white men were skeptical of the accusations of Mayella Ewell, the daughter of poor, white "trash." They believed, Lee implies, that the accusation against Robinson grew out of poisoned relations between blacks and poor whites rather than out of attempted rape. The judge and prosecuting attorney at trial made their opinions clear. Scout noticed throughout the trial that Mr. Gilmer, the prosecuting attorney, did not give the case his best effort. Atticus Finch, after the trial, commented on the attitude of the judge towards the Ewells: "John [Taylor, the judge] made [Bob Ewell] look like a fool. . . . John looked at him as if he were a three-legged chicken or a square egg. Don't tell me judges don't try to prejudice juries." Despite the jury's apparent certainty of Robinson's guilt, Atticus Finch thought it likely that Robinson's conviction would be over-turned on appeal. One might surmise that, given the different, class-based opinions about Robinson's guilt, had he not at-tempted to escape, as his guards claimed, he probably would not have been executed by the state. Class and gender tensions clouded issues of race and suggest that not all whites believed black men accused of assaulting white women should invari-ably pay with their lives. The possibility that guards staged Robinson's escape in order to mask their vigilante justice un-derscores this point.

Fiction Versus Reality

Comparing fictional narratives with actual events, though use-ful, is complicated. Although fictional situations rarely con-form exactly to actual events, Harper Lee's exploration of race, class, and gender relations in a small southern town exposed how racial prejudice produced irrationality among whites, ul-timately depriving African Americans of justice. As Atticus said, "people go stark raving mad when anything involving a Negro comes up." *To Kill A Mockingbird* suggests that social prejudices, attitudes, and beliefs, controlled primarily by race and class attitudes, determined justice. Lee makes a valid ob-servation: justice was emphatically not color blind in the seg-regated South. And many black men lost their lives after being accused, some of them falsely, of sexual assault by white women.

Accepting the notion that the course of events was un-swerving—that "Tom was a dead man the minute Mayella Ewell opened her mouth and screamed"—obscures a more complex reality. Cases of black-on-white sexual assault, rather than revealing a rigid color line, illuminate how the interaction of race, gender, class, and sexuality were defined by and continually redefined racial relations. Historians, by confining their analyses to spectacular resolutions of interracial conflict—lynchings and infamous cases like that in Scottsboro, Alabama, in 1931 [when nine black teenagers were accused of raping two white girls]—have implied that ideas about race alone propelled white southerners' reactions to charges of interracial crime. . . .

In *To Kill a Mockingbird*, Atticus Finch chided his son, Jem, for wondering why the jury did not give Tom Robinson a prison sentence rather than the death sentence by saying, "[He's] a colored man, Jem. No jury in this part of the world's going to say, 'We think you're guilty, but not very' on a charge like that." Despite Atticus Finch's stated belief, [real-life] evidence . . . shows that white juries made such determinations most of the time. [While past] cases indicate that whites involved in trials initially appeared to be united by race, . . . requests for pardon reveal [that] whites were not always united by their common whiteness and were willing to consider issues of gender or class alongside issues of race.

The Africanist Presence in *To Kill a Mockingbird*

Diann L. Baecker

Diann L. Baecker is a professor of languages and literature at Virginia State University.

The theme of race, and specifically the "Africanist presence," is muted both externally and from within To Kill a Mockingbird. *Externally, both literary scholars and teachers of the novel, instead of focusing on racial themes, often give precedence to such subjects as Boo Radley, the townspeople, the metaphor of the mockingbird, and Jem's maturation. Internally, Lee herself minimizes the importance of race in her novel, especially by decentralizing or even altogether silencing the African voice. But muted or not, the Africanist presence very much permeates* To Kill a Mockingbird, *just as it permeates America's cultural context.*

The racial themes of Harper Lee's *To Kill a Mockingbird* are acknowledged by literary scholars at the same time that they discuss the novel as though it mainly concerns Boo Radley or Atticus Finch, an impression which the author herself helps to create. Because it is routinely taught to high school students, the novel deserves greater scrutiny than it has received. As with *The Adventures of Huckleberry Finn*, where the metaphor of the river is often given prominence over the issue of slavery in the novel, *To Kill a Mockingbird*'s place in the high school canon has been finessed by minimizing the importance of its racial themes.

In her 1992 book *Playing in the Dark* Toni Morrison suggests several areas in American literature that warrant further

Diann L. Baecker, "Telling It Black and White: The Importance of the Africanist Presence in *To Kill a Mockingbird*," *The Southern Quarterly*, vol. 36, spring 1998, pp. 124–132. Copyright © 1998 by the University of Southern Mississippi. Reproduced by permission.

study. One of them is the theme of the Africanist character as an enabler, as a vehicle by which

> the American self knows itself as not enslaved, but free; not repulsive, but desirable; not helpless, but licensed and powerful; not history-less, but historical; not damned, but innocent; not a blind accident of evolution, but a progressive fulfillment of destiny.

In Lee's novel of a small southern town, the Africanist presence is muted in spite of the prominence (paradoxically) of the trial in which an innocent black man stands accused of the rape of a young white woman. Nevertheless, within the novel itself the African American characters enable the town of Maycomb, Alabama, to define itself. Viewed as part of the literary canon, at least as it is introduced to high school students, *To Kill a Mockingbird* also illustrates the way in which literature works to illustrate and define the values of a society. Some scholars have worked very hard to deny the importance of the African American characters in the novel while they accept the portrait of a white society these characters make possible. This article will attempt to foreground the role in the novel of the Africanist characters, as defined by Morrison, in the development of the identity of all the inhabitants of Maycomb County. It will also attempt to shift the focus back from such themes as the Gothic ones or the maturation of Jem, to the issue of race. . . .

Comparisons with *The Adventures of Huckleberry Finn*

Parallels between [*The Adventures of*] *Huckleberry Finn* and *To Kill a Mockingbird* are worth noting. . . . On one level, Mark Twain's story of a boy, a raft, and a runaway slave resembles Lee's tale of a young girl and the town recluse whose eventual reemergence into society is facilitated by the false accusation of a black man of the rape of a white woman. Both novels have southern settings and child narrators. Both, in some ways, contain critiques of class and race. However, because of a combination of formal properties within the text and social properties in the way the novels have been placed within the literary tradition, both books illustrate the ways in which racial critiques can be minimized and made more palatable.

The critique of race is muted, in part because of the use of a child narrator. In [*The Adventures of*] *Huckleberry Finn* this serves to hide the ideological assumptions of the society and culture it describes. On the one hand, we believe that Huck offers us an unfiltered view of his society because he lacks the cynicism and corruption of an adult. On the other, it is easy to dismiss Huck precisely because he is a naif already marginalized and without status in society and, thus, to dismiss the critique as the oversimplifications of a child. [*To Kill a*] *Mockingbird* is also narrated by a young child whose view of her society is both honest and naive because she lacks the perspective of an adult. We can accept the fact that she believes the most important event of that summer is Boo's appearance, not the trial and the eventual death of Tom Robinson at the hands of prison guards, and by accepting her point of view we, too, can downplay the significance of the racial tensions described in the novel. Moreover, both books are taught as children's stories (or, more precisely, novels suitable for adolescents) although both were written for adult readers. Clearly, [*The Adventures of*] *Huckleberry Finn* and *To Kill a Mockingbird* are novels which adults may feel nostalgic about but which they are not meant to take seriously, being, as they are, "children's" books.

Literary Reviews Dismiss Race Issue

The presence of a child narrator and society's relegation of each to "children's" literature seems to have made these books less about race in the prevailing culture. Reviewers in the 1950s helped canonize [*The Adventures of*] *Huckleberry Finn* by ignoring the sociological and ideological implications, at best [glossing] over the racial themes in the novel [*To Kill a*] *Mockingbird*'s entry into the canon was similarly finessed by contemporary reviewers. Edwin Bruell brings up the comparison to Twain's novel in his review of [*To Kill a*] *Mockingbird* published in 1964. He cites with approval Twain's preface in which he threatens to prosecute anyone searching for a motive, moral, or plot in the novel. Bruell tells us that he, too, has his own "private comments on theme hunting, moral seeking, and symbol chasing" in novels. [*To Kill a*] *Mockingbird*, he tells us, is about the townspeople, not about Robinson. Here is a man who definitely envisions his audience as white, male and, at the very least, middle-class. He not only tells us that Lee "write[s] like a woman" and that Mayella Ewell is the kind of backwoods character who "rape[s] easily," but he also denies Tom Robinson his manhood, describing him repeatedly as being "bewildered," "misunderstanding," "innocent," and "harmless," adjectives frequently applied to Twain's Jim [the escaped slave in *The Adventures of Huckleberry Finn*] as well. This, then, is Bruell's conception of a novel which shines a "[k]een scalpel on [r]acial [i]lls".

Edgar H. Schuster, writing in 1963, also feels that too much emphasis is placed on the racial themes of the book. He complains that students "stress the race prejudice issue to the exclusion of virtually everything else." Operating on the assumption that those parts which are given the most attention in a novel are the most important, he counts the pages given to the trial and concludes that they constitute only "fifteen percent of the total length of the novel." In his opinion, "any interpretation that regards the whole first half of a novel merely as prologue and the last tenth as epilogue is in dire need of refinement." Moreover, since the two children, in his opinion, are relatively free from any form of racial prejudice and since the issue of race is concentrated in one part of the book only, he believes that the racial issues do not even properly qualify as a "motif." Schuster believes that the five primary themes of the book are Jem's maturation, the social stratification of the town, the metaphor of the mockingbird, education, and superstition. He gives the last two primary importance. Schuster believes that Lee's achievement lies not in the fact that

> she has written another novel about race prejudice, but rather that she has placed race prejudice in a perspective which allows us to see it as an aspect of a larger thing; as something that arises from phantom contacts, from fear and lack of knowledge; and finally as *something that disappears* with the kind of knowledge or "education" that one gains through learning what people are really like when you "finally see them." (emphasis added)

This notion that education makes racism "disappear" is a common myth. Racism is commonly ascribed to poor white trash, as though those of the middle and upper classes (who possess more education) have nothing to do with it. Schuster's vision of the relative unimportance of race in the novel is as unrealistic as the idea that racism disappears with education. Schuster does, however, ask an interesting question about the novel. If this book is, indeed, about race relations why, he wonders, does it devote so little time to the trial? This is a question I will come back to, but here it is worth pointing out that there is no one-to-one correspondence between a theme's importance and the number of words devoted to it.

It might be suggested that these articles are typical only of early-1960s academic scholarship which, perhaps, reflects the determination of academia to hold onto its ivory tower image in the face of the onslaught of the civil rights movement and certainly reflects the formalist stranglehold on literature at a time when the physical properties of a work—such as the number of words devoted to a particular theme—took precedence. However, one of the most recent and extensive works on [*To Kill a*] *Mockingbird* also diminishes the racial theme. Claudia Durst Johnson's *To Kill a Mockingbird: Threatening*

Boundaries is based on a 1991 article she wrote about the legal and extra-legal boundaries of the novel. She calls [*To Kill a*] *Mockingbird* a "study of how Jem and Scout begin to perceive the complexity of social codes" and "tale about variety of boundaries—those of race, region, time, class, sex, tradition, and code." Despite its promise to explore boundaries, the book subsumes any notice of the racial themes of the novel under discussions of the legal code, the Gothic romance, or the theme of the mockingbird. When Johnson does mention race, it is generally only in passing. Like so many scholarly works before it, *Threatening Boundaries* remains more formalist criticism than social critique.

Lee, Too, Minimizes Race

If contemporary scholars sometimes minimize the importance of race in the novel, it is small wonder, considering the fact that the author does so, too. As more than one reviewer has pointed out, Lee's novel begins and ends with Boo Radley. [*To Kill a*] *Mockingbird* opens with the following words by the author/narrator:

> When he was nearly thirteen, my brother Jem got his arm badly broken at the elbow. . . . When enough years had gone by to enable us to look back on them, we sometimes discussed the events leading to his accident. I maintain that the Ewells started it all, but Jem, who was four years my senior, said it started long before that. He said it began the summer Dill came to us, when Dill first gave us the idea of making Boo Radley come out.

Thus, Jem's broken arm becomes the result not of the act of a racist man, but a childhood game to lure Boo Radley from his home. The trial of Tom Robinson is a significant part of the book, even if the trial itself occupies only fifteen percent of the novel. What may be more significant than the number of pages devoted to the actual trial may be the way in which Lee has constructed the novel so as to compress the issue of race into a tightly constrained portion of the book, bounded on either side by tales of Boo. The Africanist presence in this novel is simultaneously illuminated and repressed by Lee. Rather than seeing this as proof that the novel is more about Boo (or Jem or Scout or Atticus) than about race, I would suggest that Lee's efforts to contain the racial element of the novel actually highlights its significance. Moreover, Boo—who frames Lee's story—may be more closely associated with the Africanist presence in the novel than is first apparent.

Boo's Connection to an Africanist Presence

In the novel Boo, a white man, is both associated with the margins and differentiated from the people who inhabit that place. He is a spook, a vampire who eats small animals and peeks in people's windows at night. He is, as Johnson has pointed out, a Gothic figure, not quite human. Never seeing the sun, he is ghostly white. There is also something grotesquely sexual about him, in the way that he stabs his father with a pair of sewing shears (a woman's tool), in the way that he is some kind of repressed child, and in the way that he lives in the womb-like darkness of his birthplace. He is part of the margins. After Jem loses his pants on the Radley fence, Scout lies in bed that night listening to the night sounds and imagining Boo at every corner:

> Every night-sound I heard from my cot on the back porch was magnified three-fold; every scratch of feet on gravel was Boo Radley seeking revenge, every passing Negro laughing in the night was Boo Radley loose and after us; insects splashing against the screen were Boo Radley's insane fingers picking the wire to pieces; the chinaberry trees were malignant, hovering, alive.

Here, Boo is associated with nature, with insects and chinaberry trees, as well as with "every passing Negro," persons also more closely associated with savage nature than with the civilizing town. As noted above, marginalized groups tend to share each other's characteristics. They collectively form the context within which they are individually placed so that women, children, and racial minorities are generally considered like each other (feminine, immature, less intelligent) as well as being dirty, uncivilized, closer to nature, and any other losing end of a dichotomy. Boo's association with insects, chinaberry trees, Negroes, and, of course, madness, helps to align him near the margins. Thus, in some ways, Boo himself is part of the Africanist presence in the novel.

Yet, as much as he lives life on the boundary of society, Boo is not like the black people or even the Ewells and Cunninghams of Maycomb. In some ways his madness makes him even more of an outcast. "A Negro," we are told, "would not pass the Radley Place at night, he would cut across to the sidewalk opposite and whistle as he walked." Black people and children, both positioned near the margin, believe; they understand Boo's nature. Yet, when it comes to offering Boo up to the legal system as well as to the sympathy and pity of the townspeople (specifically, the townswomen who cannot be counted upon to do what the men consider to be right for Boo), the matter is taken care of in the best small town way. Boo, by virtue of being white and of a good family, is given special consideration. Just as his father was allowed to keep him home rather than seeing his son sent to jail or a reformatory after his teenage rebellion, the sheriff and Atticus decide to administer their own extra-legal justice; Bob Ewell, they decide, dies by falling on his knife, not at the hands of Boo Radley.

While Boo crosses boundaries of white and black, culture and madness, borrowing characteristics of the Africanist presence while retaining ties to the white townspeople, other members of Maycomb's community are more definite about their identity. Jem articulates the viewpoint of the townspeople by noting that there's four kinds of folks in the world. There's the ordinary kind like us and the neighbors, there's the kind like the Cunninghams out in the woods, the kind like the Ewells down at the dump, and the Negroes. . . . The thing about it is, our kind of folks don't like the Cunninghams, the Cunninghams don't like the Ewells, and the Ewells hate and despise the colored folks.

Townspeople's Identities

The townspeople, as Aunt Alexandra points out, may all have "streaks"—to drink, to madness, to intermarriage—but they are not, first of all, white trash. Unlike the Cunninghams, the townspeople do not live in the woods or suffer from "entailments." Unlike the Ewells, they do not live "behind the town garbage dump in what was once a Negro cabin." They do not drink up all their money so that they must be allowed to hunt out of season so their children do not go hungry. Most importantly, while they may marry their cousins, they do not molest their own daughters. There is nothing particularly remarkable about these facts. "[H]e's a Cunningham" is all the explanation Scout believes the new schoolteacher should require. Mr. Ewell's incestuous relationship with Mayella, the driving force behind her desire to make loving contact with someone else, even if that person is a black man, is mentioned only in passing in the novel. On the other hand, the "warm bittersweet smell of clean Negro" or a black chauffeur "kept in an unhealthy state of tidiness" are facts remarkable enough to be noted. The incestuous relationship of a white trash man with his white trash daughter is a part of the novel often glossed over by scholars who probably find it unremarkable anyway, as if to say, what else can be expected from people living so close to Negroes.

Part of the manner in which the townspeople distinguish themselves from others is through language, both the ability to read and the ability to name, abilities which fall out along racial lines. Naming is especially important in distinguishing black from white. While we know Tom's last name, he is most often referred to in the novel by only his first. Calpurnia is just "Calpurnia" as is her son, Zebo. In addition to names, the mark of literacy is an important distinction which serves to cut off the townspeople from both the black residents and the poor whites. The Ewells and the Cunninghams take their children out of school after a year or two (if that long), while Scout can read before the first grade. Much is made of Calpurnia's literacy and the fact that she has "two languages," one which she uses to other black people at her church and the other which she uses at the Finch home. She has taught her son to read, also, and it is he who leads the singing in church by lining the hymns, a practice fascinating to the hyperliterate Finch children.

If the townspeople form their identities by setting themselves apart from what and who they are not, it is even more important for people like the Ewells. Poor whites in the South owned little more than the color of their skin which served to both form an identity with the class above them and to distinguish them from the black people they tried hard to keep beneath them. The only way Bob Ewell is any better than his black neighbors is that, if "scrubbed with lye soap in very hot water, his skin [is] white". By taking advantage of a "quiet, respectable, humble Negro," however, he comes close to losing even this distinction. As Atticus tells Jem, the white man who cheats a black man is trash, no matter "how fine a family he comes from". Atticus's harsh judgment stems from the fact that the white man and the black man are not perceived as being equal. Taking advantage of an ignorant, humble Negro is like kicking a dog or taking candy from a child; it is capitalizing on your superior position. It is simply not done—at least not openly.

Maycomb's Marginal Citizens

Those on the margin share not only questionable hygiene, but a more animalistic sexuality as well. For example, there is something sexual about Boo's madness. He is a child trapped in a man's body, a man who supposedly drinks the blood of animals and prowls around in the dead of night. His sexuality is frozen in adulthood. The black population of Maycomb, as well as the Ewells who live so close to them, have a much more potent sexuality, a sexuality which the townspeople with their powder and propriety try to avoid. Scout's fascination with the trial may be less related to her love of her father as to her growing awareness of her gender, a gender she shares with the powerless Mayella. In the novel, Atticus is called a nigger-lover because he defends Tom. It is extraordinary that he would take the word of a black man against a white man and that he does so forms the impetus for Bob Ewell's murderous rage. What is not treated as extraordinary in the novel is the alleged crime itself, just as the incestuous relationship of a white trash man with his white trash daughter is unremarkable. In the same sense, the brute sexuality of the black race is taken for granted. As Atticus states in his closing arguments, the Ewells are counting on the jury to understand that black men cannot be trusted around white women. In truth, it is Mayella who is literally a nigger-lover and her crime is as monstrous as Robinson's alleged one. In fact, it is the sole motivating factor for the trial.

It is Mayella who saves seven nickels over a whole year's time so that she can send all of her siblings to town for ice cream and, thus, have the house to herself when she invites Robinson in. *She* kisses *him* and, worse, is caught doing so by her father. After beating her, he goes to town and charges Robinson with rape. The novel states that Mayella's subsequent testimony in court is motivated by guilt:

> She has committed no crime, she has merely broken a rigid and time-honored code of our society, a code so severe that whoever breaks it is hounded from our midst as unfit to live with. . . . She must destroy the evidence of her offense. . . . She must put Tom Robinson away from her. Tom Robinson was her daily reminder of what she did. . . . She was white,

and she tempted a Negro. She did something that in our society is unspeakable: she kissed a black man.

What is speakable, what is spoken and then dismissed as irrelevant and unimportant, is that Mayella's rape has come at the hands of her father. As she tells Tom, "what her papa do to her don't count". Her testimony is motivated less by shame than by fear—not of Robinson, but of her father. Atticus calls her a victim of "cruel poverty and ignorance," but what she is most clearly a victim of is incest and physical abuse. What motivates her scheme—which, again, takes her an entire year to put into practice—is the desire to be touched with love rather than violence.

It is during the trial scenes that a minor character makes his appearance who, like Boo, blurs acceptable social boundaries. The implications of his actions are much more serious, however, and he makes an appearance in the novel only to quickly recede again. Dolphus Raymond is the town scandal, always "drinkin' out of a sack." He lives a scandalous life, "way down near the county line" where he resides with a "colored woman and all sorts of mixed chillun." It is the opinion of the townspeople that these children must be "real sad" because they belong nowhere, being neither black nor white. Interestingly, while Lee offers no contradiction to the opinion that Mayella has sinned gravely by kissing a black man, Dolphus's character is portrayed as far more sympathetic. A few pages later in the novel, he offers Dill a sip from his sack in order to settle the child's stomach, and it is then that Dill and Scout learn that Dolphus is only drinking coca-cola. He pretends to be drunk in order to give the townspeople a reason for his behavior. Clearly it is more scandalous for a white woman to kiss a black man, than for a white man to openly live with a black woman. There are, however, other implications, not the least of which is the suggestion that this character appears and disappears so quickly because Lee finds the topic of interracial love compelling yet impossible to talk about. In addition, it is interesting to note that she carefully articulates Dolphus's status in the community. Dill observes that Raymond "doesn't look like trash" and Jem is quick to explain that he is not. In fact, "he owns all one side of the riverbank down there, and he's from a real old family to boot." Like Boo, Raymond can finesse his position between borders by virtue of his unquestionable position within white society.

Significance of the Africanist Presence

Lee is able to talk about issues of gender, particularly sexuality, because of the metaphorical nature of the Africanist presence in the novel. In addition to Mayella, Boo, and Dolphus Raymond, there is Atticus: he is almost Christ-like both in his devotion to what is good and true and in his virginal asexuality. He has been widowed for a number of years, but never even dates another woman. Atticus's relationship to Calpurnia is also interesting. She, too, is apparently widowed (there is a son for whom there was presumably once a father, but there is no mention of a husband). When his sister wants her fired, Atticus defends Calpurnia, noting what a big part of the family she is. While she sleeps in the kitchen when she spends the night at the Finch home, she nevertheless fulfills all the functions of a wife in 1930s Alabama—she cooks, cleans, disciplines the children, and essentially provides for the Finch family as if it were her own. Thus the Africanist presence can function as an enabling metaphor for discussing not only racial identity, but issues of gender and class as well. The process of identification made possible by the Africanist presence allows Lee's female protagonist to safely explore issues of sexuality, issues which seem to touch neither her nor her family directly. Within a larger context, it functions as the not-me which allows the rest of us—black and white, male and female—to find our relative position in society.

Formalist criticism is often valuable in itself. I do not believe any literary scholar, no matter what his/her theoretical leanings, is immune to a well-turned phrase. Scout's simple greeting—"Hey Boo"—will always resonate for me when I think of this novel. But literature is so much more than beautiful phrases or well-crafted plots, especially when it is part of high school education. Whatever else literature can be, it remains a cultural artifact and the way we talk about a novel—or teach it—is significant. Because, as Morrison demonstrates, the Africanist presence is part of the cultural context of America, its influence can be found in American literature, even in places where we think it is not or where it has spilled over the carefully measured boundaries we have delineated for it.

Contending Voices in
To Kill a Mockingbird

Theodore R. Hovet and Grace-Anne Hovet

Both Thedore R. Hovet and Grace-Anne Hovet are professors emeriti of the University of Northern Iowa. The former is the author of Master Narrative: Harriet Beecher Stowe's Subversive Story of Master and Slave in *Uncle Tom's Cabin and* Dred.

To Kill a Mockingbird *is celebrated for shedding light on the Jim Crow South's "disease" of racism. But the sometimes violent and always oppressive racism shown toward blacks of the time was part of a larger system of oppression, one controlled by white patriarchy, or more specifically, middle-class white men. As well as one could witness the cruel injustice and prejudice shown toward Tom Robinson, one could observe sexism inflicted upon Scout and class bigotry toward the Ewells.*

Through contending voices within the novel, a link between racism and gender/class oppression is clearly identified.

To *Kill a Mockingbird* remains an important work because Harper Lee insistently undermines typical assumptions in the United States about the origins of racism. Rather than ascribing racial prejudice primarily to "poor white trash" [according to Annalee Newitz and Matthew Wray], Lee demonstrates how issues of gender and class intensify prejudice, silence the voices that might challenge the existing order, and greatly complicates many Americans' conception of the causes of racism and segregation. . . .

[*To Kill a Mockingbird*'s] powerful critique of racism and its sophisticated use of established elements of the American

Theodore R. Hovet and Grace-Anne Hovet, "Fine Fancy Gentlemen and Yappy Folk: Contending Voices in *To Kill a Mockingbird*," *Southern Quarterly*, vol. 40, fall 2001, pp. 67–78. Copyright © 2001 by the University of Southern Mississippi. Reproduced by permission.

literary tradition such as the "coming of age" or "initiation" formula, the American Gothic, and classic realism—in other words, its wedding of social relevance to literary aesthetics—make it both a "readerly" and a "teacherly" work. To borrow the words of Roy Hoffman, "Long Lives the Mockingbird"

It also has in recent years gained increasing critical respect. Once dismissed by influential critics such as Stanley Kauffmann and Brendon Gill as sentimental, static, and intellectually dishonest, *To Kill a Mockingbird* has been praised recently by Claudia Durst Johnson, Janice Radway, Dean Shackelford, and Carolyn Jones for its literary complexity, its vivid evocation of character and setting, and its powerful critique of racism and patriarchy. We fully concur with these recent critical assessments, believing that the novel and the movie are two of the finest accomplishments in mainstream American culture. We also feel that because of the work of these critics it is unnecessary to mount yet another defense of the aesthetic and intellectual quality of the novel. Instead, we want to look at the way Lee uses the voice of the narrator and the voices of other characters that contest that narration in order to better understand the way the novel links racism to gender and class oppression. . . .

Class Conflicts Within Racism

Published in 1960 and filmed in 1961, *To Kill a Mockingbird* appears at the moment when the nation, pushed by an aggressive civil rights campaign led by the NAACP [National Association for the Advancement of Colored People] and changing socioeconomic and political conditions (we should not forget that the Cold War made racial discrimination an international embarrassment and a potent propaganda tool for anti-American forces), was attempting to make the watershed transition from legal segregation in most of the South and socially sanctioned segregation throughout much of the nation to a commitment to racial equality in deeds as well as words. The school desegregation decision of the Supreme Court (*Brown v. Topeka Board of Education*) appeared only six years before publication of the novel and the federal assault on racial inequality (the 1964 Civil Rights Act) was still several years in the future. In short, *To Kill a Mockingbird* was written and published amidst the most significant and conflict-ridden social change in the South since the Civil War and Reconstruction [a period following the Civil War (1865–1877) when former Confederate states were controlled by the federal government before being readmitted to the Union]. Inevitably, despite its mid-1930s setting, the story told from the perspective of the 1950s voices the conflicts, tensions, and fears induced by this transition. The middle-class narrative voice in *To Kill a Mockingbird* which is so appealing to most readers articulates what would become one of the dominant arguments of southern progressives, one uncritically echoed by many northern liberals. What some might see as virulent southern racism, the narrator tries to tell us, is not characteristic of the South as a whole but was created and sustained by a backward element in the rural South represented in the novel by the Ewell clan. Unable or unwilling to employ modern agricultural practices or to educate themselves and their children in modern forms of labor, this "white trash" mistakenly blames its increasingly marginal position in society on the intrusion of African Americans who will not accept their secondary social status. As one of the whites in *To Kill a Mockingbird* puts it, "it's time somebody taught 'em a lesson, they . . . gettin' way above themselves." Moreover, Scout explains, these rural whites blame the increasing presence of African Americans on the more prosperous white leadership in the towns—"those bastards who thought they ran this town," to quote Bob Ewell. For this reason, the narrator would have us believe, the unjust treatment of African Americans like Tom Robinson is not the fault of the leaders of southern society like her father, the judge, and the newspaper editor. It is the product of an uneducated and irresponsible class of poor whites who use physical intimidation and mob rule to defend what little status they have left. From her vantage point in the late 1950s, the narrator of *To Kill a Mockingbird* implies that this group is an anachronism [that] will disappear in the wake of an emerging industrialized and urbanized "New South." The Atticus Finches will then assume their rightful leadership positions and begin creating a more just society. The narrator's strategy of placing responsibility for American intolerance and injustice on the vanishing rural poor—what we can call "the white trash scenario"—was so successful that it has become a cliché in popular culture, evident not only in *To Kill a Mockingbird* but also in films like *Easy Rider* and in prime time television programs such as *[In the] Heat of the Night* and *I'll Fly Away*.

This is not to say that the narrator and other southern apologists were completely disingenuous. The virulent racism of rural whites helped maintain Jim Crow, [and] fueled the resistance, often violent, to the Civil Rights Movement. . . . The attempt by southern apologists to assign this group the primary responsibility for racism in order to exonerate middle- and upper-class whites, however, is a false reading of history. As C. Vann Woodward pointed out during the early stages of the southern civil rights movement, American imperialism and its slogan of "the white man's burden," along with Supreme Court decisions in the 1890s supporting segregation, implicated the nation as a whole in racist policies. Despite this reality, nevertheless, the white trash scenario worked because the accused were a natural scapegoat. Mostly uneducated and without voice in the media, desperately poor and without economic influence, poor rural whites were helpless to counter the negative stereotype created by the southern apologists and perpetuated by the national media. The were demonized into "the other" by civil rights advocates and progressive southerners. "Poor whites," conclude Annalee Newitz and Matthew

Wray in their analysis of white trash, "are stereotyped as virulently racist in comparison with their wealthier counterparts. As long as the poor are said to possess such traits, people can convince themselves that the poor should be cast out of mainstream society." ...

Voices Silenced by White Patriarchy

Ironically, Lee's desire to create a realistic portrayal of a southern region unmasked the strategy of the southern apologists, including her own. In order to make southern racism understandable, she not only used the techniques of realism and regionalism, but she also created a double plot, the stories surrounding Boo Radley and Tom Robinson. Several influential critics such as W. J. Stuckey and Harold Bloom maintain that the two stories are a result of artistic failure, an inability to create an organically developed narrative. But, as Claudia Johnson has demonstrated, the double plot opens the text to a more profound reading than one would expect from Lee's use of the "coming of age" or "beset American justice" formulas. Johnson points out that by placing the story of the children's reactions to "Boo," the Finch's neighbor, whom the town thinks is mentally impaired, alongside the town's response to Tom Robinson, Lee makes concrete the psychology of racism. More specifically, Scout and Jem's construction of "Boo" as a gothic monster, an "other" that embodies the mysterious outside forces that constantly threaten the known world of home and family, suggests that white southern society has also constructed the African American as an "other," a monster, who supposedly threatens the established order. Just as Scout and Jem must grow up by confronting the gothic monster of their own and the town's creation, Johnson's reading contends, so must southern society confront the racial monster that it has constructed.

Scout's struggle to come to terms with the reality behind "the other" inevitably sensitizes her to voices silenced by white

A family of sharecroppers is pictured in Alabama in 1935. Many whites in the Great Depression–era South were very poor. This may have driven some to especially strong racism against African Americans as a way of maintaining a sense of superiority. Walker Evans/ Hulton Archive/Getty Images.

patriarchy. Guided by these voices, Scout—and the attentive reader—become aware that racism is part of a general pattern of exclusion and oppression which must be overcome before anyone can be said to be free. *To Kill a Mockingbird*, John Burt notes, begins as a "story about race and turns into a story about class."

In keeping with the white trash scenario, the adult Jean Louise Finch places the responsibility for racial injustice squarely on the shoulders of a socioeconomic group without power or voice in the South—the poor, uneducated, disease-ridden rural whites represented by Bob Ewell. He falsely accuses Tom Robinson of raping his daughter, Mayella, whom he himself has physically and sexually abused, and tries to destroy Atticus for his defense of a "nigger." At the same time, the adult narrator disassociates from these events the leadership of the town represented by her father (a respected lawyer and longtime state legislator), the judge who presides over Tom's trial, and the local newspaper editor. But if we pay close attention to the narration as it shifts from the adult Jean

Louise's omniscient point of view to the first-person account of events by the young Scout, we hear a voice whose story of experience with exclusion and oppression creates gaps and contradictions in the story that the adult is trying to tell. First of all, Scout draws attention to the fact that the points of conflict in the narrative are marked by the absence of a female presence, particularly the maternal. Mrs. Finch, Mrs. Ewell, and Mrs. Radley have died before the key events in the story. Thus there are no mothers who have participated in Boo's confinement, implicated themselves in Mayella's abuse by her father, or exonerated Atticus's failure to act more decisively in the state legislature to combat segregation and lynching. Moreover, much to Scout's indignation, women are not allowed to serve on juries in Alabama. Consequently, they are not implicated in the wrongful conviction of Tom Robinson. . . .

Maycomb's inability or unwillingness to hear Scout's individual voice [because she is a young girl living in a sexist time and place,] causes her to be acutely sensitive to more subtle kinds of silence generated by white patriarchy. Her saintly father, Atticus, has served in the state legislature most of his adult life and even after defending Tom Robinson is re-elected without opposition. He presumably has had and will have opportunity to voice his opposition to racial injustice. However, Scout faithfully records how the seemingly courageous liberal is plagued by a strange inability to speak its name, i.e., racism, using instead words without any clear referents like "something" or "it." For example, in trying to explain to Jem why the jury found Tom Robinson guilty, he says that the members "saw something come between them and reason. . . . There's something in our world that makes men lose their heads—they couldn't be fair if they tried." The unnamed "something" is further mystified by his frequent use of "it": "Don't fool yourselves—it's all adding up and one of these days we're going to have to pay the bill for it. I hope it's not in you children's time."

Hierarchy of Hatred

Atticus's inability to name "the disease" is symptomatic of his failure to combat racism in Maycomb and in the state legislature. When Jem tells his father that because of Tom's unjust conviction he must "go up to Montgomery and change the law," Atticus responds: "You'd be surprised how hard that'd be. I won't live to see the law changed . . ." In summary, Atticus is eloquent in defending the law but is silent concerning the racism which brought Tom to trial and conviction. The narrator also draws our attention to still another kind of silence of well-intentioned men like Atticus. Those who have only seen the movie probably are unaware that in the novel Bob Ewell's attack on Jem and Scout is motivated as much by class hatred as by the desire to avenge Atticus's defense of Tom. They certainly would not be aware that in the novel Atticus himself is implicated in this virulent classism. As reported by his daughter, he has a hopelessly inaccurate conception of the social structure of Maycomb. Despite his law practice, which makes him relatively affluent, and a long tenure in the state legislature that gives him social prestige, he identifies himself as "poor" and as a member of the humble and decent "common folk." By using this term, he hides his privileged status and positions himself to characterize people like the Ewells as uncommonly indecent. They are "animals" rather than human beings crippled by generations of poverty and disease. Thus in the Maycomb envisioned by Atticus there are only two classes of whites: the decent common folk and those "yappy" or "tacky" people, as Jem calls them, who are "not our kind of folks." As with his inability to do more than identify racism as "it," Atticus's response to this group is to treat them as unredeemable. Scout explains the Finch view of "white trash":

> Every town the size of Maycomb had families like the Ewells. No economic fluctuations changed their status—people like the Ewells lived as guests of the county in prosperity as well as in the depths of the depression. No truant officers could

keep their numerous offspring in school; no public health officer could free them from congenital defects, various worms, and the diseases indigenous to filthy surroundings.

One result of this attitude on the part of men like Atticus is to construct for these poor whites the same kind of segregated space that has been constructed for the blacks. Their poverty forces them to live only in a "dump adjacent" to the "colored quarters." . . .

Because of this systematic exclusion from the life of the community, Ewell's false accusation that Tom raped his daughter must be read as more complex than a simple act of racism. Ewell is also attempting to break out of the social isolation that has been imposed upon him and his clan by mainstream society in Maycomb. Atticus admits to Scout and Jem that Ewell accuses Tom in the hopes of playing upon the racism of the "respectable" people in order to raise his status in the town. In this he succeeds in so far as the white townspeople support Tom's conviction. But at the same time he fails to overcome the class structure that has held him in poverty. Atticus explains that the judge made Ewell "look like a fool" and treats Ewell "as if he were a three-legged chicken or a square egg." "He thought he'd be a hero," Atticus concludes, "but all he got for his pain . . . was, okay, we'll convict this Negro but get back to your dump." As the narrator puts it, "Maycomb gave them Christmas baskets, welfare money, and the back of its hand."

This comment makes clear that Scout is attaining a more realistic view of the Ewells than that propounded by her father. She is putting into practice Atticus's advice—"to climb into his skin and walk around in it." By so doing, she perceives and reports to her readers that Ewell does not see the social structure of the town in the same way as Atticus. He identifies the common people with those like himself who are held down by a wealthy white ruling class (Atticus's "common folk") who manipulate African Americans in order to keep poor whites like himself in their place. In breaking into Judge Taylor's house or attacking the Finch children, Ewell attempts to strike back at "those bastards who thought they ran this town." In short, much of the injustice and violence that occurs in the novel originates in a society obsessed with class as much as race. As Jem notes, the region is not composed of decent common folk and animals, but of a hierarchy of hatred: "our kind of folks don't like the Cunninghams, the Cunninghams don't like the Ewells, and the Ewells hate and despise the colored folks." Lee's novel, therefore, verifies the contention of Newitz and Wray that "as a stereotype, white calls our attention to the way that discourses of class and racial difference tend to bleed into one another, especially in the way that they pathologize and lay waste to their 'others.'" . . .

Overcoming Contradictory Voices

Lee's effort to provide a realistic portrait of a small southern town subverts her employment of the white trash scenario and destabilizes the patriarchal foundation on which it rests. In so doing, the narration liberates a medley of voices that articulate a widespread pattern of exclusion and oppression in a typical southern town. First of all, the retrospective nature of Scout's coming-of-age saga focuses on her gradual recognition of "justice beset" and offers hope that race, gender, and class barriers can be broken down. Scout's persistence in speaking directly to the poor white Walter Cunningham about his legal problems leads to the dispersal of a mob attempting to lynch Tom; her willingness to humanize "the other" (Boo) by inviting him into her own life interjects a feminine desire for inclusion that challenges a society completely controlled by the fathers who had virtually imprisoned him for his difference; her recognition of the humanity of Mayella reveals the artificiality of a class structure that would dehumanize difference. In spite of Lee's overt use of the despicable white trash scenario, her story ends up destroying that strategy and exemplifying the observation of Judith Fetterley that the best regional fiction written by women includes "the story of one previously silenced and marginalized," thereby affecting "the definition of margin and center" and "calling into question the values that produced such definitions."

But like so much else in this rich novel and movie, the voices remain elusive and contradictory. In spite of the critique of patriarchy, little seems changed in Maycomb. Towards the end of the novel, Scout points out to Jem the contradiction of her teacher hating Hitler for persecuting the Jews while at the same time declaring that the conviction of Tom was justified because "it's time somebody taught 'em a lesson, they were gettin' way above themselves." Rather than supporting her viewpoint, Jem, who now identifies with the adult male world, silences her, screaming, "I never wanta hear about that courthouse again, ever, ever, you hear me? You hear me? Don't you ever say one word to me about it again . . .!" The reader who has adopted a critical position toward the town leaders will clearly interpret this scene as Lee's conclusion that the town is returning to the racist, classist, and sexist norms which prevailed in this typical southern community before Tom Robinson's fateful encounter with Mayella Ewell, and that it will try to silence anyone who advances any viewpoint that challenges those standards. As Scout observes, "Jem had acquired an alien set of values and was trying to impose them on me."

But the attentive reader will also be inspired by another factor. Despite the downward pull to conformity that the "common folk" in Maycomb exert—especially Aunt Alexandra, Jem, and Dill—the adult Jean Louise will not be silenced. Her discovery of her own voice trumpets her power as adult narrator to challenge the hegemony [the authority of a dominant group over others] of community norms that oppress and exclude individuals on the basis of race, class, and gender.

To Kill a Mockingbird: A Paradox

Eric J. Sundquist

Eric J. Sundquist is a professor of English at UCLA and author of many books and articles on southern literature, including To Wake the Nations: Race in American Literature; The Hammers of Creation: Folk Creature in Modern African-American Fiction; *and* Strangers in the Land: Blacks, Jews, Post-Holocaust America.

By addressing America's age-old hatreds through the idealized eyes of children, To Kill a Mockingbird *remains one of the twentieth century's greatest models of paradox. These hatreds were embodied in the book's setting, the Jim Crow South, which used white womanhood as a primary argument for segregation: if blacks were integrated into white society, what would happen to white female "purity"? This fear kept both blacks and women in their subordinate places.*

Tom Robinson represents a history of black men falsely accused of sexual misconduct against white women. The child characters in To Kill a Mockingbird *represent hope for change for America's Tom Robinsons.*

Given its enduring appeal to deep wells of white American innocence, it may seem at first glance surprising how blunt is *To Kill a Mockingbird*'s examination of the South's "rape complex," as Wilbur Cash once called it. As a portrait of the South of the 1930s, the novel might be taken simply as a confirmation of the archetypal defense of lynching offered in the Senate by Alabama's J. Thomas Heflin: "Whenever a negro

Eric J. Sundquist, *The South as an American Problem*, Athens: University of Georgia Press, 1995. Copyright © 1995 by the University of Georgia Press. Reproduced by permission.

crosses this dead line between the white and negro races and lays his black hand on a white woman he deserves to die." It could better be argued, however, that the appeal of the book, whose story is focused, after all, on the psychological and physical maturation of a young white girl with whom readers of the 1950s and 1960s are expected to identify, lies in its portrayal of a contemporary episode of the southern sexual "disease" and in its invocation of the specter of "mongrelization [mixing of races]" that was once more appearing in the oratorical and editorial protests that fueled southern reaction to *Brown v. Board of Education* [the 1954 Supreme Court decision that ended school segregation]. Behind the veneer of Scout Finch's first-person naïveté, Lee's novel defies, without destroying, conventional white southern fears of black sexuality, which drove the South, said Lillian Smith [an antiracist Southern writer born in 1897], to super-impose the semiotics of Jim Crow upon the white female body: "Now, parts of your body are segregated areas [that] you must stay away from and keep others away from. These areas you touch only when necessary. In other words, you cannot associate freely with them any more than you can associate freely with colored children." Smith's characteristically acerbic description of the ethos of segregation brings together the two strong vectors of Lee's novel—its focus on childhood, the battleground of desegregation, and the rhetorical power of white womanhood, long the weapon of choice in racist arguments against equality.

Throughout the South *Brown* [*v. Board of Education*] provoked new hysteria of the sort recorded in Mississippi circuit court judge Tom Brady's infamous broadside "Black Monday" (so called for the day the *Brown* [*v. Board of Education*] opinion was issued), in which he summoned up the specter of alien invasion ("Communism disguised as 'new democracy' is still communism, and tyranny masquerading as liberalism is still tyranny") and prophesied that desegregation would unleash a new black threat to "the loveliest and the purest of

God's creatures ... [the] well-bred, cultured Southern white woman or her blue-eyed, golden-haired little girl." Sedition and the threat of racial corruption were everywhere: the year before Lee's novel was published, an Alabama state legislator who objected to the plot of a children's book entitled *The Rabbit's Wedding*, in which a white rabbit marries a black rabbit, succeeded not only in banning the subversive book from state libraries but in having copies burned as well. Against the grain of its ineffable [unspeakable] goodness *To Kill a Mockingbird* includes as well this powerful undertow of southern resistance and, in its half-disguise of violent racial realities, inscribes in an equally dangerous children's story the nightmare of America's own growing up.

History's Impact on *To Kill a Mockingbird*

The capital rape case of Tom Robinson tried by Atticus Finch occurs in 1935, set in a small-town Alabama courtroom that would inevitably have been reverberating with the impact of the ongoing trials of the young black men known as the Scottsboro Boys. Perhaps the most notorious modern criminal trials with race not technically but nonetheless fundamentally at issue, the ordeal of the young men charged with the rape of two white women, in a sequence of trials lasting from 1931 to 1937, put the South under sensational national scrutiny matched only by that aroused by the 1955 murder in Money, Mississippi, of Emmett Till, a fourteen-year-old Chicago boy accused of being fresh with a local white woman. Although it is conceivable that Lee's character Tom Robinson was inspired by the death sentence given a real-life black Alabama man named Tom Robinson in 1930 for his part in defending his family from a lynch mob, a story recounted in Arthur Raper's *Tragedy of Lynching*, actual parallels to Tom's case were readily available, and Scottsboro was only the most egregious evidence that the kinds of justice administered by southern mobs and southern courts were often indistinguishable. From the southern point of view Scottsboro was a call to arms. Vander-bilt historian Frank Owsley, for instance, identified the Yankee intrusion into the sacred body of the South prompted by Scottsboro with the prior infamies of abolitionism and Recon-struction, when radical whites had encouraged black men "to commit universal pillage, murder and rape." Outside the South, though, Scottsboro was emblematic of southern injus-tice and a litmus test of sectional paranoia, as was the Till case a generation later.

With mounting tension over civil rights activism aug-mented by the exoneration of Till's white killers, *To Kill a Mockingbird* was written, and subsequently read, in an atmo-sphere charged on the one hand by the impact of *Brown* [*v. Board of Education*] and on the other by publicity about the revival of Judge Lynch in the South. Yet by dwelling on the narrative recollection of time past—"when enough years had gone by to enable us to look back on them," Scout tells us in setting the context for the book's action on the first page—the plot deliberately casts backward to the era of Scottsboro, and Lee could easily have replaced her own epigraph from Charles Lamb ("Lawyers, I suppose, were children once") with Lang-ston Hughes's "The Town of Scottsboro," one of several poems he devoted to the cause:

> Scottsboro's just a little place: No shame is writ across its face—Its court, too weak to stand against a mob, Its people's heart, too small to hold a sob.

Hughes's Scottsboro might as well be Maycomb, where Tom Robinson is tried and quickly sentenced to death, or Sumner, Mississippi, where Till's murderers were tried and just as quickly acquitted. This doubled legal time frame is but one of several ways in which Lee, like Mark Twain before her, lays one era upon another in the retrospective narrative of Scout Finch, who looks back to a time when "people moved slowly . . . took their time about everything," when "there was no hurry, for there was nowhere to go." Scout's nostalgia tells us about the operation of temporality in autobiography, about Lee's share in the long southern tradition of antimodernism, and about the power of mourning, commingled with defiance, in the reservoir of southern memory. But it tells us, more to the point, that we are reading at every moment an allegory of the South's own temporality and its public philosophy of race relations: "Go slow."

Romanticizing a Bygone South

To Kill a Mockingbird is a novel of childhood, but one saturated in narrative consciousness of deeper regional and national time. Although it is not, strictly speaking, a historical novel, its careful deployment of familial genealogy, state history, and the romantic stereotypes of southern "breeding" create a context in which the pressure of contemporary time, with its threatened destruction of a white southern way of life, becomes urgent. The novel harks back to the 1930s both to move the mounting fear and violence surrounding desegregation into an arena of safer contemplation and to remind us, through a merciless string of moral lessons, that the children of Atticus Finch are the only hope for a future world of racial justice. Framed by the Boo Radley story, the book's racial "nightmare" is to a noticeable degree made peripheral for young readers to the gothic tale of the "malevolent phantom" Boo and the revenge of Bob Ewell. But Boo Radley's story is at the same time a means to displace into more conventional gothic territory the Finch children's encounter with "blackness" as it is defined by the white South and, more broadly, by white America. Associated from the outset with animal mutilation and black superstition, and with the laughter of Negroes passing in the night, Boo functions transparently as a harbinger [something that foreshadows what is to come] of violated taboos and a displaced phantasm of racial fear, ultimately unmasked as the gentle, domesticated "gray ghost" of harmonious integration. The novel's concluding Halloween se-

quence, with its brilliant prelude of the school pageant devoted to Alabama history and personified products of Dixie
agriculture (dressed as a ham, Scout survives Bob Ewell's
attack), tells us that the true danger comes from "white trash"
("Boo" evolves into the insidious "Bob"); and it offers the illu-
sion that racial hysteria—the Klan, night-riding mobs, the
White Citizens Council—can be likewise unmasked, humiliated, and brought to justice once the South disposes of its
childish fears and moves forward into the post-*Brown* [*v.
Board of Education*] world.

To Kill a Mockingbird is a masterpiece of indirection that
allows young readers to face racism through the deflecting
screen of a frightening adventure story, just as it allows American readers to face racism through a tale that deflects the
problem to the South. Embedded in an episodic story of wit
and charm, and pursued through a series of remembered
events that often channel serious racial issues into a puzzle of
half-truths, children's games and pranks, and devious piety,
the novel's lessons are as often held in abeyance as they are
driven home by Lee's analogical strategies and her temporal
displacement of the book's action into the lives of a pre–
Brown [*v. Board of Education*] generation. From the very outset of the novel Scout's reminders that we are reading a tale of
the Depression-era South have the effect of suspending our
judgment. The New Deal [President Franklin Roosevelt's 1930s
programs that promoted economic recovery], however it may
have helped southern blacks economically, posed little challenge to Jim Crow; though key civil rights legislative and judicial policy dates from the decade, the practice of segregation,
and often of mob rule, remained largely untouched by the
awakening of southern liberalism.

There is thus everywhere available to the reader as an explanation of the book's dramatized racism and miscarriages of
justice the argument that its action belongs to a bygone era.
One effect of the temporal displacement, in fact, is to anchor

Fourteen-year-old Emmett Till was killed after allegedly whistling suggestively at a white woman in Mississippi. His murderers were acquitted of the crime, but later sold their story of the killing to Look *magazine. The murder and trial were national news while Harper Lee was working on* To Kill a Mockingbird. *AP Images.*

the novel's social crises in a remembered world of general economic deprivation and cultural isolation. The Finch family is comparatively well off, of course, but the region's impoverished small farmers and sharecroppers, whether black or white, live still in the "shadow of the plantation," to borrow the title of Charles Johnson's important study of Black Belt Alabama in the 1930s, "dulled and blocked in by a backwardness which is a fatal heritage of the system itself." Indeed, *To Kill a Mockingbird* itself so clearly harks back to the tradition of liberal exposés of southern racism, whose classic texts may be dated from the 1930s—works such as Johnson's *Shadow of the Plantation* (1934), Raper's *The Tragedy of Lynching* (1933), John Dollard's *Caste and Class in a Southern Town* (1937), Wilbur Cash's *The Mind of the South* (1941), and climaxing in a book with an even broader canvas, Gunnar Myrdal's monumental *An American Dilemma* (1944)—that the novel might almost be read as a kind of [summary] recapitulatory tribute to the tradition. Be that as it may, *Brown v. Board of Education* irrevocably changed things, and any novel dating from the rising crest of the civil rights movement must bear the consequences of its own nostalgia for a simpler, slower time, especially when that nostalgia is as tightly interwoven with the narrative's moral fabric as in the case of *To Kill a Mockingbird*. . .

Atticus: A (Liberal) Man of the South

Atticus Finch has been studied by attorneys for the quality of his moral character, and his cinematic portrayal by Gregory Peck as a man of great tenderness and justice is so ingrained in American consciousness as to make him nearly impossible to imagine otherwise. If there is little question as to Atticus's integrity, however, his actions and his defense of Tom Robinson are seldom seen in any sort of historical context; and his own participation in the book's evasion of the hardest moral questions is usually ignored in favor of his commanding pedagogy [the art of teaching]. It is surely not hard to imagine that Atticus Finch, whether as portrayed by Peck or not, would be more easily recognized than Thurgood Marshall [the first African American to serve on the Supreme Court] by the vast majority of Americans. Presented as the southern "good father" standing as he does in nearly mythic contrast to bad public fathers such as George Wallace [former pro-segregation Alabama governor], Ross Barnett [former Mississippi governor and member of the Ku Klux Klan], and Orval Faubus [former Arkansas governor who was a leader in anti-segregation movements after *Brown vs. Board of Education*], Atticus is depicted as a grand hero to the book's black community, who stand in silent reverence as he passes from the courtroom after his futile but heroic defense of Tom.

Atticus Finch is a good lawyer, then, and a gentleman, but he is not a crusader. He takes Tom Robinson's case because he is appointed counsel (as required by 1930s statute in Alabama capital cases), is a man of professional ethics, and appears, moreover, to believe in defending Tom, even though he has no illusions about winning a rape case involving a black man and a white woman. Atticus ends his defense of Tom Robinson with a ringing declaration that the court of Maycomb County has available to it the same measure of justice one might seek from the United States Supreme Court—"in this country our courts are the great levelers, and in our courts all men are created equal," he reminds his jury—but there is never one moment of doubt as to the verdict that will be returned. Scout puts it best: "Tom was a dead man the minute Mayella Ewell opened her mouth and screamed." Against the certainty of defeat, Atticus Finch's heroic effort is all the more moving. In his integrity, humility, and common sense, Atticus is almost certainly meant to provide an alternative to the cranky fulminations [thunderous verbal attacks] about "Sambo [an anti-black caricature depicting blacks as eternal children content in their servitude]" states' rights, and the Cold War voiced by [writer William] Faulkner's liberal attorney, Gavin Stevens, in *Intruder*

131

in the Dust [the story of a black farmer accused of murdering a white man]. At the same time, however, Atticus too remains a man of the South, a moderately liberal insider. How else could he function as the symbolic conscience of his family and the white townspeople, those "with background" who privately "say that fair play is not marked White Only," who wish him to do the right thing on their behalf, but who otherwise scorn him as a "nigger-lover," who excuse themselves from jury duty, thus turning the decision over to "white trash," and who uphold at all human cost the grandiose myth of southern white womanhood?

Southern Trappings

The course of Tom's ordeal and Atticus's defense is artfully constructed to exacerbate two mirroring paradoxes. First, Tom is placed in a deadly trap when he must either give in to Mayella Ewell's sexual advances or resist her, and then when he must either recant his story or accuse a white woman of lying. Driven to the impudence of declaring his fear that, no matter what he does, he will end up the victim of a judicial system in which mobs and juries are indistinguishable—"scared I'd hafta face up to what I didn't do," he meekly but archly replies to the prosecutor—Tom is the personification of the daily apprehension that [psychologist and social scientist] John Dollard found to be widespread among southern African Americans in the 1930s: "Every Negro in the South knows that he is under a kind of sentence of death; he does not know when his turn will come, it may never come, but it may also be at any time." The second paradox, which is Scout's, the reader's, and finally the book's, is perfectly summed up in Atticus's admonition to his daughter, who has sought to defend him from the scorn of town and family alike: "[T]his time we aren't fighting the Yankees, we're fighting our friends. But remember this, no matter how bitter things get, they're still our friends and this is still our home." The peculiar political morality that pervades the novel is incarnate [embodied] in this expression of near paralysis, which at once identifies the race crisis as a *southern* problem—a matter of states' rights, ideally immune to renewed federal intervention—and describes it in terms that make decisive local action unthinkable. Even though Atticus Finch's own heroism may work to obscure this element of the book's lesson, the novel is, in fact, perfectly in accord with the southern view that the meaning of *Brown* [*v. Board of Education*] was to be worked out internally. Just as the South closed ranks against the nation at the outset of desegregation—a reaction heightened by Mississippi's being thrust into the national spotlight by the Till case—so *To Kill a Mockingbird* carefully narrows the terms on which changed race relations are going to be brought about in the South.

Atticus's moral courage forms a critical part of the novel's deceptive surface. Whether to shield his children from the pain of racism or to shield Lee's southern readers from a confrontation with their own recalcitrance [stubborn defiance]; Atticus, for all his devotion to the truth, sometimes lies. He employs indirection in order to teach his children about Maycomb's racial hysteria and the true meaning of courage, but he himself engages in evasion when he contends, for instance, that the Ku Klux Klan is a thing of the past ("way back about nineteen-twenty"), a burlesque show of cowards easily humiliated by the Jewish storeowner they attempt to intimidate in their sheeted costumes purchased from the merchant himself. Such moments are not distinct from the book's construction of analogies for moral courage in the face of ingrained communal racism—for example, Atticus's killing of the rabid dog or Mrs. Dubose's breaking free of her morphine addiction—but rather part of it. Indirection and displacement govern both the novel's moral pedagogy and, in the end, its moral stalemate. The ethical example of Atticus Finch is heightened in exact ratio to the novel's insistence that, so far as Maycomb and Alabama are concerned, it is both inimitable [matchless] and incomplete.

In the wake of losing Tom Robinson's case, Atticus suffers personal anguish and bitterness, but he reminds the children on this occasion and others that both juries and mobs in every little southern town are always composed of "people you know," of "reasonable men in everyday life" of "our friends" and that racial injustice is a southern problem that must be solved from within by right-thinking white people. Atticus does not characterize the verdict as "spitting on the tomb of Abraham Lincoln," nor does he say of the jury: "If you ever saw those lantern-jawed creatures, those bigots whose mouths are slits in their faces, whose eyes pop out like a frog's, whose chins drip tobacco juice, bewhiskered and filthy, you would not ask how they can do it." These remarks, which belong to Samuel Leibowitz, the principal defense attorney in several of the Scottsboro trials, cut through the decorous sanctimony of *To Kill a Mockingbird* and constitute as sharp an intervention into the novel as the comparable public reaction, outside the South, to the exoneration of the murderers of Emmett Till. . . .

Hypothesis of Desegregation

Tom Robinson's disabled arm is his legal alibi, but it is also the author's alibi—in the one case useless but in the other, for that very reason, perfect. Atticus must not only speak for him but also appropriate into his own ethical heroism Tom's masculinity and dignity as a black man, his very identity, much as the book itself appropriates Tom's African American world to the ethical heroism of its white liberal argument. The reiterated moral of the novel—that to understand a person you must stand in his shoes or, better yet, "climb into his skin and walk around in it"—is, in fact, called into question by its principal strategy of representation, which is in turn bound tightly to the limited, ventriloquized voice that African Americans are granted in the legal and customary world of the novel that belongs as much to 1950s America as it does to 1930s Alabama. *Powell v. Alabama* [1932 Supreme Court decision] gave criminal defendants the right to legal representation as passionate and valuable as that afforded Tom Robinson by Atticus Finch. But in its very assault on states' rights and, by implication, on the doctrine of segregation, *Powell* [*v. Alabama*] also underlined the fact that the triumph of white liberalism might not be the end of racism.

It was Harper Lee's fortune to write at a moment when white America was ready for fictive salvation, and the risk she took cost her widespread scorn in the South for betraying her region and its way of life; but it was also her fate to write at a moment when other voices were being heard—in boycotts and demonstrations, in demands for enforcement of the law—and when other options for literary representation of the struggle for black justice were readily apparent. Just as the reach of Atticus Finch's integrity is circumscribed by his admonition that moral action must respect the prejudices of "our friends" and ultimately abide by local ethics, so the novel's undeniable power is circumscribed by its own narrative strategies.

It is no mistake, perhaps, that the white children of *To Kill a Mockingbird* never grow up. In Scout's retrospective narration, they remain ever poised for the hypothesis of desegregation. With the promised land of the post–*Brown* [*v. Board of Education*] world ever on the horizon, Scout and Jem are timeless inheritors of the liberal vision even as Atticus Finch is its timeless exponent. Yet in choosing to contain Tom's story—the story of the black South—within the carefully controlled narrative consciousness of Scout and the idealized grandeur of Atticus Finch, Lee subordinated lasting vision to a moral expediency that remains familiar enough in late-twentieth-century America, as the racial problems of the South have become more commonly recognized as national problems. Locked into the paired narrative capacities of Atticus and Scout, Tom Robinson, and the social and historical African American world for which he stands, are left without a true voice in their own representation, living still, in every reread-ing of the novel, under the South's death sentence and return-ing us to the admonition of James Baldwin in his essay on Faulkner and desegregation: "Any real change implies the breakup of the world as one has always known it, the loss of all that gave one an identity, the end of safety. . . . There is never time in the future in which we will work out our salva-tion. The challenge is in the moment, the time is always now."

Learning Good Judgment in the Segregated South

Thomas L. Shaffer

Thomas L. Shaffer is a professor of law at the University of Notre Dame. He has written about To Kill a Mockingbird *in two of his books:* American Legal Ethics *and* Faith and the Profession.

Historically, southern white womanhood has been the rationalizing factor in segregation and racism. It was the driving force behind the prosecution—and attempted lynching—of Tom Robinson in To Kill a Mockingbird. *The idealized and pure female also becomes the model of behavior for young southern girls, such as Scout. Aunt Alexandra epitomizes the teacher of this model. Yet it is from less gender-conventional role models— Atticus, her forward-thinking father; Calpurnia, their black servant; and Miss Maudie Atkinson, their open-minded neighbor— that Scout learns her greatest lessons. It is through these individuals that Scout learns about justice, principles, and good judgment.*

"I am the sum total of those who preceded me," [author] Elie Wiesel wrote recently, "and so are you. Am I responsible for what all of them have done before I came into this world? No. But I am responsible for what I am doing with the memory of what they have done."

Jean Louise Finch (Scout), her brother Jeremy, their summer friend Dill, who comes to them from Meridian, Mississippi, and their school friends from the town and the farms around Maycomb grew up in memory and learned, or failed

Thomas L. Schaffer, "Growing Up Good in Maycomb," *Alabama Law Review*, vol. 45, winter 1994, pp. 1–9. Copyright © 1994 *Alabama Law Review*. Reproduced by permission.

to learn, and accepted, or refused to accept, responsibility for what they did with the memory and in the name that memory gives to a place.

These children in Maycomb learned the virtues before they learned that what they had learned were virtues. The virtues they learned were virtues formed in the memory and in the name that the memory gives to a place. They grew up good in Maycomb. Their childhood story, told in large part as a story about their father Atticus, is about growing up in virtue. The epigraph [quotation found at the beginning of her novel] Harper Lee chose for the novel is from Charles Lamb: "Lawyers, I suppose, were children once." And the dedication of the novel is to Miss Lee's father, a Monroeville lawyer ("to Mr. Lee"), and to her sister, who became a lawyer ("and Alice"), and it is framed as if it were copied from a warranty deed in Atticus Finch's law office ("in consideration of Love & Affection").

Growing Up a Lady

A slightly quaint example of growing up good in Maycomb is Scout's learning to be a Southern Lady, told most directly in the chapter that describes the meeting of a group of Maycomb's Methodist ladies in the Finch home. It is one of the few occasions on which Scout wears a dress rather than bib overalls, which is significant as well as symbolic: Throughout the story, Atticus's and Calpurnia's failure to put Scout in dresses is evidence of their failure to train her to be a lady.

Scout's Aunt Alexandra, temporarily taking charge of the home in order to correct the failure and to provide what a single-parent male and a black woman could not be expected to provide, is hostess for the meeting of the missionary circle of the Maycomb Alabama Methodist Episcopal Church South. She recruits Scout and Calpurnia to help her entertain the members, who gather there to discuss the wretched condition of the children of polygamous [having more than one wife] and polytheistic [worshipping multiple gods] Africa. Scout goes about her duties with reluctance: "Ladies in bunches always filled me with vague apprehension and a firm desire to be elsewhere . . . a feeling . . . Aunt Alexandra called being spoiled."

As if to confirm Scout's misgiving, the young girl has hardly sat down to sip her lemonade when Miss Stephanie Crawford from across the street asks her if she wants to grow up to be a lawyer like her father. "Nome, just a lady," Scout answers, and Miss Stephanie says that if Scout wants to be a lady she will have to wear dresses more often. Miss Maudie Atkinson, from a different house across the street, secretly intervenes to teach Scout a lesson—or to confirm her in it—on the importance of meeting slight insults with quiet dignity: "Miss Maudie's hand closed tightly on mine, and I said nothing. Its warmth was enough."

This becomes a lesson in judgment as much as a lesson in behavior, as, a few minutes later, Mrs. Merriweather begins idly to berate her absent black servant and Miss Maudie stops the conversation with a caustic comment. The secret hand-squeeze was a lesson in quiet dignity, but the lesson in judgment is that silence is not always the virtuous response; sometimes a lady stands up against evil, in this case the customary racism that Atticus, elsewhere in the story, refers to as "Maycomb's usual disease."

Lessons in Judgment

How is a lady-in-training to know when judgment—what the moral philosophers call prudence—requires speaking out, and when judgment requires quiet dignity? The way ladies tell the difference, as Scout sees it at the meeting, rests on, or at least is confirmed by, an understanding about allies. The fact that morally influential others are present and supportive makes it possible to confront ordinary evil. All through this story, collaborators in the good describe the distinction between ordi-

nary evil and casual insult. In Tom Robinson's case and
Atticus's confrontive, uncivil defense of Tom Robinson, this
looking around for allies becomes clear when Atticus learns
that Braxton Bragg Underwood, publisher of the *Maycomb
Tribune*, was standing by to defend him from the mob that
had come to the jail at night to lynch Atticus's client. At another point in the story, Atticus senses that the judge in the
Robinson case is an ally because he seems sympathetic with
the unpopular tactic Atticus has chosen for his client's defense. The judge seems to have appointed Atticus to defend
Tom Robinson because he hoped for and expected just such
an unpopular choice of legal theory for the courtroom.

Scout, however, who learns about truth and courage from
her father and from Mr. Underwood and Judge Taylor, has to
learn to practice prudence as a lady among ladies. Scout learns
that, among ladies, there is a sisterhood of sympathy and
principle that does not operate in dramatic encounters such as
the ones Atticus has with the mob in front of the jail, or with
the racist prosecutor in the courtroom, or the mad dog in the
street. Among ladies, the presence of collaborators in virtue is
as quiet as Miss Maudie's handsqueeze.

Southern Lady Sisterhood

Collaboration occurs when Miss Maudie stops Mrs.
Merriweather's ruminations on Southern black people with a
caustic remark (which also operates as a defense of the unusual racial politics of the Finch house). After the remark,
Scout notices a silent and unexpected alliance between Miss
Maudie and Aunt Alexandra. The alliance is unexpected because the two women are not friends; they have seemed to
Scout to be operating at cross purposes as Miss Maudie insists
on being mildly unconventional and, worse, on supporting
whatever Atticus does, in his house or out of it. By contrast,
Aunt Alexandra is as uncomfortable with what Atticus is doing for Tom Robinson as most white people in Maycomb are,

and is persuaded that Atticus and Calpurnia are raising Scout to be unladylike. Despite what Scout has already seen to be cold courtesy between Miss Maudie and Aunt Alexandra, what Scout sees after Miss Maudie silences Mrs. Merriweather is a compact to protect the Finch house (and Atticus too). From this compact arises a bit of unexpected sisterhood that teaches Scout about the way Southern ladies get together when they have to without surrendering the independence that keeps them apart:

> [Aunt Alexandra] gave Miss Maudie a look of pure grati-
> tude, and I wondered at the world of women. Miss Maudie
> and Aunt Alexandra had never been especially close, and
> here was Aunty silently thanking her for something. For
> what, I knew not.... There was no doubt about it, I must
> soon enter this world, where on its surface fragrant ladies
> rocked slowly, fanned gently, and drank cool water.

And then the crisis of Tom Robinson's persecution and the gentle drinking of cool water meet. Atticus comes in the house, away from his office at an unusual time of day. He does not interrupt the meeting, except that his presence has already in-terrupted it. He asks Aunt Alexandra and Miss Maudie to speak with him in the kitchen; he tells them that Tom Robin-son has been killed by his jailers and he asks Calpurnia to go with him to the Robinsons' home because he needs her to help him tell the new widow what has happened.

No one tells the other ladies at the meeting what has hap-pened. No doubt that is because Atticus, his sister, and his neighbor know (and Scout learns) that decency requires that the widow learn first. And so the meeting, the fans, the rock-ing, and the cool water, go on as if nothing has happened—except that Scout and Aunt Alexandra have to take over Calpurnia's duties as well as their own. Scout then describes her duties: "I carefully picked up the tray and watched myself walk to Mrs. Merriweather. With my best company manners, I asked her if she would have some. After all, if Aunty could be a lady at a time like this, so could I." ...

Calpurnia's Teachings

Calpurnia, Scout and Jem's surrogate mother, is the person in the story who is, no doubt, Atticus Finch's best friend (although he would, in a small town in Alabama in 1935, not have put it that way). Calpurnia is a demanding teacher. She is the mistress of what feminist scholars, looking at our culture's moral past, call "the woman's sphere." She is the one who teaches these white children, as Aristotle said, the moral virtues and good habits, long before they choose to behave well— long before their virtues are virtues. Much of what the women in Scout's life think the children learned from their father they in fact learned from Calpurnia. Atticus exemplified and confirmed intellectual content, and added the right names—classical names, such as truth, courage, justice—to what they already knew and had begun, because of Calpurnia, both to practice and to choose to practice.

Calpurnia demands, nourishes, and comforts. "By watching her," Scout says, "I began to think there was some skill involved in being a girl." When Scout criticizes Walter Cunningham for putting syrup all over his lunch (in Maycomb it's called dinner), after Jem induces Walter to come home from school to eat with the Finches, Calpurnia is an avenging angel on behalf of Walter and of Southern manners: "Yo' folks might be better'n the Cunninghams but it don't count for nothin' the way you're disgracin' 'em—if you can't act fit to eat at the table you can just set here and eat in the kitchen!" But when Scout is in pain over the hypocrisy and drudgery of public education, Calpurnia is a comforter, she makes crackling bread and gives it to Scout, as a surprise, after school. She also tells Scout she missed her: "The house got so lonesome 'long about two o'clock I had to turn on the radio." And Scout concedes some softening: "Calpurnia's tyranny, unfairness, and meddling in my business had faded to gentle grumblings of general disapproval. On my part, I went to much trouble, sometimes, not to provoke her."

Calpurnia's Community

When Aunt Alexandra comes to Maycomb to see to Scout's refinement, the first thing she wants to do is send Calpurnia away. Atticus bears most of Alexandra's reforms with patience; when, for example, she tells Scout that Scout has to be a sunbeam in her father's life, he tells Scout (on the side) that the Finch family already has enough sunbeams. But he is openly stubborn when it comes to his friend Calpurnia. He identifies her as a kinswoman: "She's a faithful member of this family and you'll simply have to accept things the way they are." He disapproves of Alexandra's well-bred practice of not saying anything controversial within Calpurnia's hearing: "Anything fit to say at the table's fit to say in front of Calpurnia. She knows what she means to this family."

Neither of these white children will ever have to live under the oppression Calpurnia lives under, although both of them will be called upon to take responsibility for what they do with the memory of old-style American racism sooner than their father—or anybody else in Maycomb—might have supposed they would. But one of the things they do have to learn—just have to—is that half the people in their town are cruelly oppressed, and it is Calpurnia's undertaking, as much as that of Atticus and Miss Maudie, to teach them about it. The fact that the children do not know, until they are preteens, that Calpurnia has a home and a family of her own justifies as much as anything in the story a nod to the irony of American history. Jem and Scout find out about both Calpurnia's family and the community of Maycomb's black Christians when they go with Calpurnia to Sunday services at First Purchase African Methodist Episcopal Church. There they also find out that the black church is the one place in Maycomb that is not racist.

The children notice that Calpurnia speaks differently among black people than she does in the Finch home (and they sharpen the contrast as they remember that "Atticus said Calpurnia had more education than most colored folks") and, being children, they mention this to her. She says it is a matter of not putting on airs. It's not that she approves of the lack of education among most of her black neighbors, nor that she thinks black illiteracy is inevitable; she has, after all, taught her own son to read from a copy of [Sir William] Blackstone's *Commentaries* [*on the Laws of England*] that she borrowed from Atticus. What the Finch children are asked to learn is that a person can work for moral gain in the community without being offensive about it: "Folks don't like to have somebody around knowin' more than they do. . . . When they don't want to learn there's nothing you can do but keep your mouth shut or talk their language."

Unconventional Teachings

Mrs. Dubose, the suffering old white bigot who lives up the street from the Finches, was left out of the movie version of the story. My guess is that the omission was not due to the economics of film making alone, but demonstrates that the movie was a 1960s civil rights story, rather than the affectionate story of an Alabama town in 1935, and that the American civil-rights agenda when Horton Foote wrote the screenplay could not find a way to come to terms with Mrs. Dubose—with the fact that Atticus Finch could endure an old woman's ruthless and racist attack on him and his client and at the same time hold her out to his children as the bravest person he ever knew, a teacher of the virtue of courage.

Mrs. Dubose was, Scout said, by unanimous neighborhood opinion, "the meanest old woman who ever lived." She so taunted Jem that he stormed into her yard and beheaded her camellias. His training as a Southern gentleman required him to apologize, make his peace with her, and spend two weeks reading to her from [Sir Walter Scott's] *Ivanhoe*. And then, when Atticus needed a way to teach his children what courage was, he dipped (a bit improperly) into his professional knowledge of her affairs and told them, after Mrs. Dubose's death, that the reading of *Ivanhoe* was to help her overcome morphine addiction, cold turkey, before she died. Her determination to die free of the addiction [that] had come upon her as beneficent professional medical therapy, on the assumption that morphine addiction is all right for old, sick people, was the lesson Atticus needed to overcome an impression he had created, in the mad-dog incident, that courage is a man with a gun in his hand. The movie leaves in the man and the gun and omits the brave old woman. The memory was just different.

Miss Maudie Atkinson teaches the children independence (I again avoid the word autonomy) and friendship. She is a devoted gardener—so much so that her ability to continue to grow flowers is a genuine consolation for her after her house burns down. But certain elements in the white Christian church in Maycomb (the Foot Washing Baptists) disapprove of her garden; it is, in their theology, a worldly indulgence. Miss Maudie is also a faithful and understanding companion for the children, as well as a source of firm support for their father in his struggle with the town in the Robinson case. It is Miss Maudie who explains the novel's title, when she tells Scout and Jem what Atticus means when he says it is a sin to kill a mockingbird. And it is Miss Maudie who defends the Finch home from the racism of Mrs. Merriweather's attack on black people. Scout says of Miss Maudie: "She had never told on us, had never played cat-and-mouse with us, she was not at all interested in our private lives. She was our friend. How so reasonable a creature could live in peril of everlasting torment was incomprehensible." Not only does Scout find out that an adult can be as much a friend as her summer companion Dill; she also learns that growing up as a Southern Christian woman includes locating and understanding theological distinctions.

Defending Southern White Womanhood

The ethos of Maycomb that clouds men's minds so badly that they will lynch an innocent black man is understood or, rather, rationalized, as the defense of Southern White Womanhood. Arthur Radley, the strange recluse who lives hidden away next door to the Finch house, and who, at the end of the story, saves the children's lives, was locked away because of an offense to Southern White Womanhood. When he was a boy he was a member of an unruly group of juveniles accused of, among other offenses, "using abusive and profane language in the presence and hearing of a female." The probate judge released Arthur (Boo) to his father, and his father locked him away.

When Atticus rushes home in the middle of the day, and interrupts the meeting of the missionary circle, after he learns that Tom Robinson has been killed, and asks Alexandra, Maudie, and Calpurnia to speak to him in the kitchen, he becomes so overwrought that he almost storms out of the room—but then checks himself, does not slam the door, and comes back briefly to make a lame joke. "I know what he was trying to do," Scout says, "but Atticus was only a man. It takes a woman to do that kind of work."

The defense of Southern White Womanhood is an attitude nourished and promulgated by Aunt Alexandra, who, Scout says, "had river-boat, boarding-school manners; let any moral come along and she would uphold it; she was born in the objective case." Hers is, though, an ethos that carries disadvantages to women—disadvantages that will be challenged, after the story ends, long before anybody in Maycomb would have predicted.

Listening to the Mockingbird

Calvin Woodard

Calvin Woodard was professor emeritus of Virginia Law before his death in 2004.

In her uniquely southern novel, Harper Lee used her writing talent to tackle racism and injustice. Her method did not involve overt speeches against racism, nor did it attack the southern laws that perpetuated racism; instead, Lee endeavored to change white values. Except for Tom Robinson's court trial, Lee, in To Kill a Mockingbird, *focused on attitudes of whites instead of injustices shown toward blacks to reach her objective.*

Two literary devices Lee used for this purpose were the "Peter Pan" factor and the "Mockingbird" factor. The former alludes to Lee's use of the child narrator, free from society's constraints. The latter involves the wide-ranging symbolism of the mockingbird, with its allusions to harmlessness, imitativeness, and triumphant virtue.

Just as I was beginning to write this Article, I found my major premise—that [*To Kill a Mockingbird*] was uniquely Southern—undercut by, of all people, Gregory Peck, the actor who had so brilliantly personified Atticus Finch in the film version of the book. In the front of my tattered paperback edition of Miss Harper Lee's classic, Mr. Peck is quoted as saying:

> The Southern town of *To Kill a Mockingbird* reminds me of the California town I grew up in. The characters of the novel are like people I knew as a boy. I think perhaps the great appeal of the novel is that it reminds readers every-

Calvin Woodard, "Listening to the Mockingbird," *Alabama Law Review*, vol. 45, winter 1994, pp. 2–7, 9–11. Copyright © 1994 *Alabama Law Review*. Reproduced by permission.

where of a person or a town they have known. It is to me a universal story—moving, passionate, and told with great humor and tenderness.

One must surely agree. *To Kill a Mockingbird* is no more about Alabama than [*The Adventures of*] *Huckleberry Finn* [by Mark Twain] is about Missouri. The tale Ms. Lee tells is a human drama that happens to be set in the rural South but transcends geographical boundaries simply because it touches upon experiences shared by persons of all races, genders, nations, and classes. Many of the deplorable conditions existing in Ms. Lee's description of Maycomb County, Alabama, during the 1930s, still prevail—and not only in the South. To a troubling degree, however, many of the regional problems Ms. Lee dealt with are now likely to be seen as national and international in scope.

Uniquely Southern Attributes

Even so, however, I still maintain that *To Kill a Mockingbird* is uniquely "Southern." Much of the book's jurisprudential [relating to the philosophy of law] value derives from its focus on the South and the failure of southern law to deal justly with nonwhites—a problem that has long plagued "Southern justice." As such, *To Kill a Mockingbird* inspired constructive changes in the South. Most obviously, it played a part in stimulating support for the civil rights movement of the 1960s and attendant changes both in the attitudes of many white Southerners and in the legal status of blacks.

It is the nature of Ms. Lee's contribution to those wider developments that I wish to address in this article. For we can glean from her effort—and particularly her approach—constructive jurisprudential insights for our continuing quest to make law the means to justice for all people.

A Literary Approach to the Problem of Racism

From a jurisprudential point of view, we can best appreciate *To Kill a Mockingbird*, and its contribution to American law, by recognizing it as an attempt by a critic of the Southern legal system to deal with a serious legal problem through nonlegal means. The serious legal problem was the shockingly unjust treatment blacks received in Southern courts.

Ms. Lee perceived law as incapable of dealing with the injustices done to blacks in Southern courts because the injustices were manifestations of a wider, more pervasive problem that affected the whole of Southern society: the ages old problem of racism. Accordingly, she was forced to look beyond law to extralegal means to address what would ordinarily be regarded as a jurisprudential problem: the functions of the legal system.

The need to go beyond law was not without precedent. In other times and places lawyers, judges, scholars, and legal critics have not hesitated, when faced with particularly knotty legal problems, to go outside law—to religion, philosophy, ethics, or the social sciences—for extralegal authority to justify legal decisions or indeed law itself. So also Ms. Lee: She differed only in that she turned to fiction, specifically to a form of children's literature, to facilitate changes that law itself seemed incapable of bringing about. Ms. Lee's use of fiction, though wonderfully fresh in the jurisprudential context of the 1950s (when she wrote), was not unusual or even uniquely Southern in other contexts.

Ms. Lee was not an "in your face" critic. She did not overtly identify racism as the problem with which she was concerned, nor did she assert her purpose to be the eradication of that problem. She did not even attack Southern law in the more conventional manner of a moral crusade against evil, usually personified by rabid Klansmen, corrupt cops, and know-nothing rednecks. Rather, in the style of a law professor teaching first year law students, she did not "lay out" her purpose. She left it to her readers to think for themselves, to draw their own conclusion by their own powers of reasoning, not by being led by the nose.

Changing White Values

The book implies that the real problem in the South was a mystery disease far more subtle and pervasive than the crude brutalities associated with the unsavory characters in the book. Indeed, the worst villains are themselves easily seen as pathetic victims of something larger and more evil than their own *venality* [being susceptible to corruption]: They are all victims of the existing social order itself; based on a hallowed tradition sustained by an elaborate network of personal relationships, custom and conventions, and ultimately enforced by law. Together, all these factors sustained a virtually invincible status quo in which racial bias was often so subtle that many white persons vehemently denied that it existed, or even that they were themselves prejudiced against blacks. Yet, whether they were or not, the cold fact remained: Blacks were held in a subhuman status.

So seen, racism in the South had two distinct dimensions: (i) a cluster of attitudes, shared by whites, which perpetuated the biased social order; and (ii) the horrid results of the biased social order—one manifestation of which was a legal system where due process of law was consistently denied to non-whites.

With the exception of the one criminal (rape) trial, however, Ms. Lee wrote about whites. She details the attitudes and habits of the white folks of Maycomb County, rather than the injustices visited upon blacks. Until the values of whites change, she seems to say, society will not change; and, as law reflects the values of society, it can do no more than uphold those values.

To Ms. Lee, "changing white values" was a banner of hope—a way of solving the American dilemma—a way of freeing the South from the dead hand of custom that held the South, and the nation, hostages to its own past.

So much for Ms. Lee's conception of the problem. Her task was a formidable one: How can one possibly hope to alter attitudes touching every aspect of life, and appearing to be as natural as the color of grass? The task she set for herself was not only intellectually difficult, but considering the nature of her purpose, and the hypersensitivity of many Southerners to any criticism of things Southern, it was also fraught with danger. Ms. Lee had good reason to be discreet in her criticisms of the South or things Southern, including Southern law.

Accordingly, the author adopted two traditional literary devices to accomplish, and simultaneously conceal, her purpose: (i) children's literature (the "Peter Pan factor"); and (ii) the free use of semimystical symbols (the "Mockingbird factor").

The Peter Pan Factor

A prominent white Southerner once observed that he could explain racial segregation to everyone except his five-year-old son. This speaker was onto a truth that helps explain the means Ms. Lee used in *To Kill a Mockingbird* to undermine the traditional racial bias built into the social order of the South. This observation suggests that, during that brief period of life called "childhood," human beings have the potential of becoming something different from adults. Many social reformers, and not only Christians, have found in the young a glimpse of a better world peopled by humans freed from social constraints of reality.

This hope and promise of the young have attracted many writers to children's literature. But alas, children grow up. I call this the "Peter Pan factor" because, as Peter Pan discovered to his dismay [in the novel by J. M. Barrie], in real life children do grow up.

Although *To Kill a Mockingbird* deals with a serious subject, it has the appearance of a children's book. As such, it follows roughly the pattern of a genre of children's literature inspired by [eighteenth-century philosopher Jean-Jacques]

Rousseau in eighteenth century France. Ms. Lee was her campaign against the race-infected social order through a fictitious young, Jean Louise ("Scout") Finch, the daughter of a lawyer from a good Alabama family. Such a child could get away with saying things no adult would dare utter. Who could possibly take umbrage [offense] at the words of a tomboy in grade school?

The Finch family lives in a pleasant, bucolic [pastoral] community [that], we learn through the children, is struggling with various problems typical of smaller communities, including public health issues, poor schools, and mental illness, all of which are exacerbated by the depression of the 1930s. Looming over the whole community is the still larger racial problem: a large population of blacks—the source of the farm labor essential to the agrarian economy—existing on the very margin of subsistence. Many of the blacks are unemployed through no fault of their own. Most of them are unskilled farm laborers and nearly all are illiterate.

These hapless blacks are natural targets of derision, cruelty, and degradation. Still, many whites are only slightly better off than the blacks they taunt. Left to fend for themselves in such a bleak situation, these underprivileged individuals, black and white, pose a potential threat to the community.

A Child's Questioning Eyes

Into this troubled world the Finch children venture. In a style [Jean-Jacques] Rousseau would have approved, the Finch children learn (through experience, not instruction) that their own beloved father is much respected by most of the townsfolk, but despised by some others. When they see and hear things they cannot understand, they turn to their father who patiently attempts to answer his children's questions in clear, rational terms. He also sternly instructs them concerning the proper reaction when reason is of no avail.

In the course of the book, Atticus teaches his children many things about law and lawyers that they learn and savor. The children also observe some things about law, and how the legal system works, that they can neither understand nor condone.

So much for the Peter Pan aspect of *To Kill a Mockingbird*. Life in a Southern town has been described, and Ms. Lee's readers have learned all they will ever know about Maycomb, Alabama, through Scout's childish eyes—meeting their neighbors, going to their school, attending missionary society teas, and observing the criminal law system at work. Scout described it all, leaving the readers to draw their own conclusions.

We realize that Scout has questions and doubts about law that even Atticus—the consummate man of law—cannot adequately explain. Where is she to look for answers? And where are we, Ms. Lee's readers, to look? Ms. Lee, like Rousseau and a good Socratic law professor, forces us to ask ourselves and to find an answer not in Southern law but in our own experience, observations, and reasoning powers.

The Mockingbird Factor

The second distinctive Southern attribute of *To Kill a Mockingbird* is the aura of mystery that envelopes it. In fact, this aura—the Mockingbird factor—seems to have the opposite function from the Peter Pan factor. The Peter Pan factor sought to illuminate the reader's understanding of the real world (Maycomb County) by revealing poignant facts, observed through the innocent eyes of a child, which adults could not see or would not acknowledge. In contrast, the Mockingbird factor was used to obfuscate [confuse], if not conceal, the author's purpose. It also defanged critics by appealing to the human pleasure that persons of all ages derive from speculating about the meaning of mysterious signs and symbols.

Although told from a child's perspective, *To Kill a Mockingbird* is not simply a child's book. It conveys the distinct impression that it is about something more. But what? As in a house of mirrors, nothing is as it seems. Everything seems to be more, or less, than it first appears to be, and something always seems to be missing. . . .

Senseless Slaughter of Songbirds

Does the finch, especially Atticus Finch, represent "law" while the mockingbird symbolizes a more elusive "justice"? Does the title imply that justice is being wantonly killed—and law is unable to save it?

In her novel, Ms. Lee refers several times to the killing of songbirds, most notably mockingbirds, and on one occasion she tells us why mockingbirds should not be killed. Here is her explanation. When the Finch children, Jem and Scout, received air rifles one Christmas, their father instructed them about shooting birds. He told them they could kill "all the bluejays you want, if you can hit em, but remember it's a sin to kill a mockingbird." However, it was left to Miss Maudie Atkinson, the Finches' free-thinking neighbor, to explain Atticus's rule to the children. "Mockingbirds don't do one thing but make music for us to enjoy. They don't eat up people's gardens, don't nest in corncribs, they don't do one thing but sing their hearts out for us. That's why it's a sin to kill a mockingbird."

The moral seems to be that it is sinful to destroy anything that makes life more pleasurable for human beings. So much for bird shooting.

Near the end of the novel, when Tom Robinson, the black man unjustly convicted of raping a white woman, was killed trying to escape from prison, Mr. Underwood, the editor of the local newspaper was outraged. He "likened Tom's death to the senseless slaughter of songbirds." Mr. Underwood expressed his anger in an editorial Scout described as follows:

"Mr. Underwood didn't talk about miscarriages of justice, he was writing so children could understand. Mr. Underwood simply figured it was a sin to kill cripples, be they standing, sitting, or escaping. He likened Tom's death to the senseless slaughter of songbirds by hunters and children." . . .

The Mockingbird As a Symbol of the Southern Mind

The mockingbird is usually called a "mocker" because it emulates the songs of other birds. Miss Lee paid tribute to the mockingbird's skill at emulating the songs of other birds in the following passage:

> "High above us in the darkness a solitary mocker poured out his repertoire in blissful unawareness of whose tree he sat in (it was Boo Radley's tree), plunging from the shrill kee, kee of the sunflower bird to the irascible qua-ack of a bluejay, to the sad lament of Poor Will, Poor Will, Poor Will."

The mockingbird's skill at emulating the songs of other birds raises several questions about the meaning of the mockingbird symbol such as: Does a mockingbird symbolize something that has no voice of its own, and therefore can only emulate others; or does it represent something that derisively mocks others?

Whatever answer given to these questions, the meaning of the mockingbird symbol must be based, at least in part, on the commonplace knowledge that the mockingbird imitates the songs of other birds with uncanny skill. Clearly, such skill requires not only intelligence but the willingness and patience to concentrate patiently on other birds long enough, and carefully enough to learn their songs by heart. It is this attribute of listening to others that suggests a particular trait associated with many Southerners, white and black.

Mockingbird Tolerance

Tolerance is not a virtue commonly associated with the South. Perhaps for that very reason, Southern parents of Miss Lee's generation attempted to instill tolerance into their children with a very heavy hand. I know because I had it drummed into my head ad nauseam in virtually the same words that Atticus spoke to his children. As Atticus said of a man that spit upon him: "You never really understand a person until you consider things from his point of view ... until you climb into his skin and walk around in it."

As noted, Atticus was in fact teaching his children the mockingbird form of tolerance: identify with, listen to, and learn from others. Since the mockingbird can emulate only that which it has listened to attentively and can only enlarge its repertoire by paying heed to (rather than imperiously dismissing from consideration) the songs of breeds different from itself, tolerance must surely be the crowning mockingbird virtue.

Is it also a Southern virtue? No and yes. For the best of reasons, the South has been characterized as intrepidly intolerant; and the need for more tolerance, especially in small, closely knit communities such as Maycomb County, Alabama, was most obvious. Miss Lee made her readers aware of that need, and her efforts have been appropriately applauded. Surely one of her messages to the white South was to cultivate the mockingbird virtue of tolerance.

From another point of view, mockingbird tolerance is not so virtuous. Undue deference to the thoughts of others is not a virtue. The mockingbird virtue ceases being a virtue when we lose ourselves in conforming to the will of others. Of course, the will of the others may be thought to be wrong, immoral, or sinful in some natural law or religious sense. Even so, we, as individuals, have a duty to ourselves to act on our own will and to be personally accountable for our actions. In this sense, we have a duty to reject the mockingbird virtue and to develop our own voices to the highest degree possible. Thus, silence may indeed be the worst sin, but emulating the songs of others is the next worst. Perhaps Miss Lee is trying to tell us that the silence of the blacks and the tendency of many whites to thoughtlessly emulate the unworthy voices of others was a particular regional problem.

In this sense, the mockingbird may symbolize a people who are not virtuously tolerant, but have compromised themselves to the extent that they have lost their own dignity as human beings by too readily acceding to and aping the will of others. Taking its songs too readily from others, society, like the mockingbird, loses its own soul. By imitating the songs of other birds for so long and so well, members of society forget their own identity and are defined not by their own individuality but by their skill at imitating others. Society literally becomes a cipher [one having no influence or value].

Mockingbird Virtue Triumphs

One might say that for many generations the blacks of the South described by Miss Lee had been reduced to ciphers. Like mockingbirds garbed in Confederate gray feathers, blacks were permitted to develop and use their voices only when, where, and how whites wanted to hear them. As a result, most black voices remained unheard, and were almost never heard as a group.

It is therefore not surprising that the biggest silence in *To Kill a Mockingbird* was that of the blacks. Except for Calpurnia, who spoke "white folks' English," we hear almost nothing from the blacks who are there. Few persons, white or black, ever heard the authentic voice of blacks, for it was stunted by a social order that had no need for it or tolerance of it. However, the blacks were there, eerily silent, and as Scout said in another connection, "exactly the same as a cold February morning, when the mockingbirds were still."

In the end however, it was the mockingbird virtue that triumphed, giving blacks the opportunity to develop their own voices and cease being mockingbirds. This victory was accomplished only through the committed work of a cadre of black lawyers, superbly trained in the mockingbird virtue of singing the songs of others. They sang the favorite songs of the American bar—such familiar songs as "justice through law," "equality before the law," and "due process of law"—with such skill they beat the white lawyers and judges at their own game.

Whether it was a black voice, a white voice, or a gray voice that won is still not clear.

Perhaps the mockingbird knows? Or Peter Pan?

Social Issues in Literature

CHAPTER 3

Contemporary Perspectives on Racism

Educational Resources Still Limited for Minorities

Neil Foley

Neil Foley is an associate professor of history and American studies at the University of Texas at Austin. His book, The White Scourge: Mexicans, Blacks, and Poor Whites in Texas Cotton Culture *won the Frederick Jackson Turner Award of the American Historical Association.*

Fifty years following Brown v. Board of Education, *which ended school segregation, African Americans continue to receive education inferior to that of whites. In addition, they are far more likely to be imprisoned in their lifetime than any other ethnic group in America. While other ethnic groups have been more widely accepted by white Americans, blacks continue to face prejudice. Even after numerous legislative attempts to improve conditions for African Americans—including affirmative action, desegregation, and equal opportunity laws—they continue to suffer from high unemployment, low wages, and high crime rates.*

With every passing decade since 1954 we continue to ask ourselves how much the South and the nation have changed since the *Brown v. Board of Education of Topeka* decision ended "separate but equal" education in public schools. The hallowed words of Thomas Jefferson that "all men are created equal," proclaimed at the nation's founding one hundred seventy eight years before *Brown* [*v. Board of Education*] seemed finally to include black men, women, and children, at least insofar as public schooling was concerned. Yet decades after court rulings ending segregation—in schools, restau-

Neil Foley, "Black, White and Brown (*Brown v. Board of Education*)," *Journal of Southern History*, vol. 70, May 2004, pp. 343–348. Copyright © 2004 The Southern Historical Association. Reproduced by permission.

rants, hotels, housing, swimming pools, and buses—the color line has hardly faded. In fact, it is beginning to look as if the line were drawn in permanent ink: black people and white people—Americans all, but still very differently situated educationally, economically, and socially. Even with massive immigration from Asia and Latin America in the last half of the twentieth century and the recent displacing of African Americans by Latinos as the nation's largest minority, we cannot seem to break free from our vision of America as fundamentally a nation of whites and blacks, with Asian Americans, Latinos, and Native Americans playing supporting roles. In many ways we remain, as [political scientist] Andrew Hacker argued more than a decade ago, "two nations," black and white, separate and unequal. The future that the *Brown* [*v. Board of Education*] decision augured and that Martin Luther King Jr. devoutly desired could only be described as a dream, given the deep divisions that separated black America from white America since the end of slavery. Yet no other court decision in our history has done more to bring an end to state-sanctioned white supremacy, to close the long era of Jim Crow, and to offer blacks the hope of achieving equality in all walks of life. That *Brown* [*v. Board of Education*] and subsequent court rulings dismantling Jim Crow have not, fifty years later, significantly narrowed the gap between whites and blacks on many fronts continues to trouble most Americans.

Laws Change, Attitudes Don't

Part of the problem has to do with the negative role blackness has played throughout our nation's history. No other group in America traces its roots to the institution of slavery, when blacks were bought and sold as the property of their white masters. After the emancipation of slaves, the enactment of the Thirteenth [which abolished slavery], Fourteenth [which gave all Americans citizen rights], and Fifteenth [which made race no bar to vote] Amendments did little to change white southerners' attitudes toward their former property, and as soon as federal troops withdrew from the South in 1877, ex-Confederates wasted little time before using local and state laws to deny blacks the very rights the newly enacted amendments were supposed to guarantee. The Supreme Court not only acquiesced in this reassertion of white supremacy (the "southern way of life" for the euphemistically inclined) but administered the coup de grace [the final blow] in 1896 when it ruled in *Plessy v. Ferguson* that separating blacks and whites on public transportation (and by implication in all public places) "does not necessarily imply the inferiority of either race to the other." The nation's highest court had shamelessly asserted that segregating blacks from whites had nothing to do with the pervasive belief in the innate inferiority of blacks, the fundamental principle of southern culture since the *antebellum era* [the period just before the Civil War]. With the exception of the *Dred Scott decision* [U.S. Supreme Court decision that stated no slave or descendant of a slave could be a U.S. citizen; it also ruled that Congress could not stop slavery in newly emerging territories of the time] in 1857, no other Supreme Court ruling had done so much damage to the cause of equality for blacks; *Plessy* [*v. Ferguson*] stood for fifty-eight years as the law of the land and was cited in hundreds of state and federal court cases as the constitutional basis for segregation in virtually all areas of life.

The Southern Way of Life

The very premise of the "southern way of life" rested on the assumption that blacks and whites could peacefully co-exist, but only if the color line were scrupulously observed where it counted the most—in the bedroom. Even before 1896, former slaveholders and state legislators (often one and the same) enacted laws to forbid black-white marriage, not only to ensure that mulattoes would have no inheritance rights that a white man was bound to respect but more urgently to prevent black men from marrying white women. Integration would lead to race-mixing, many white southerners believed, which for them always meant black men seeking the sexual favors of white women. On the one hand, interracial marriage was—and still is—the single greatest transgression against white supremacist ideals. Interracial sex, on the other hand, was as southern as cornbread and collard greens, at least as far as the sexual appetite of white men for black women was concerned. We are all by now familiar with the family feud between the black and white descendants of Thomas Jefferson and his house slave, Sally Hemings. The author of the Declaration of Independence and a Founding Father of the United States was almost certainly the not-so-proud father of black children, and his white descendants are loathe to acknowledge a common bloodline with their black cousins. In the same tradition, seventy-eight years ago J. Strom Thurmond, the arch-segregationist and Dixiecrat who was elected to the Senate in the same year as the *Brown* [*v. Board of Education*] decision, fathered a black daughter, Essie Mae Washington-Williams (whom the media consistently refers to as "biracial" rather than black, a racial promotion intended perhaps to soften the blow to Thurmond's family). In 1925, when he was twenty-two years old, Thurmond seduced Carrie Butler, a sixteen-year-old house maid (although to the media in 2004 it was an "affair"—not sexual exploitation), and until his death in 2003 at the age of one hundred he repeatedly denied that he had fathered a black child. No doubt Strom Thurmond is a relic of the past, but it was always understood among white men in the South, from Jefferson to Thurmond, that the strict separation of blacks and whites was to be observed only from the waist up.

Whiteness a Property Right

To reflect on the *Brown* [*v. Board of Education*] decision is to reflect on the whole of southern history, since from the era of slavery until relatively recent times the South has forcefully resisted the enfranchisement [freeing] of its black citizens. Other regions of the nation, the North in particular, were often little better (and sometimes worse) in recognizing the constitutional rights of blacks, but the genealogy of white supremacy has its deepest roots in the Deep South. White supremacy never had as firm a grip on the rest of the nation, which had to contend with massive immigration from southern and eastern Europe between 1880 and 1920 and from Asia and Latin America after World War II. Many of the European groups—Italian, Polish, and Jewish—passed through periods of intense discrimination before transmuting into Caucasians through the racial alchemy of a melting pot that excluded blacks, Asians, and to a lesser extent American Indians. Black American citizens, orphaned by their own government, suffered the humiliation and deep disappointment of watching wave after wave of immigrants learn to negotiate the color line by distancing themselves from blacks. Immigrants moved into the urban ghettos, took jobs once held by blacks, and moved out of the ghettos. Always left behind, blacks had few allies in either government or the private sector to defend African American interests. Since slavery, blacks were accustomed to looking after themselves, but it rankled nonetheless when immigrants fresh off the boat had opportunities that blacks did not.

After 1965 the United States witnessed a massive influx of immigrants, primarily from Asian and Latin American countries and particularly from Mexico, and political attention shifted briefly from the problem of urban black joblessness and poverty to that of undocumented immigrants. In an outburst of anti-immigrant hysteria in California in 1994, voters passed a referendum, Proposition 187, that sought to deny medical and educational services to undocumented immigrants, mainly from Mexico, and their children. Almost half of all blacks in California, fearing economic competition from Mexican immigrants, voted for the proposition. Twelve years earlier, in a highly publicized murder, two white autoworkers in Detroit attacked and killed Vincent Chin, a Chinese American, in part because of their identification with other white autoworkers who had lost their jobs as a direct result of the growing competition from Japanese car imports. That Chin was not Japanese was not as important as his being Asian and therefore "foreign" and a threat. While not going to the violent extremes of some whites, many blacks nonetheless blamed immigrants for the loss of their jobs and frequently shared the belief that the government did more to protect the rights of immigrants than of some citizens. Despite periodic eruptions of anti-immigrant hysteria over the last few decades, whites nevertheless tend to mingle and mix more readily with Latinos and Asian Americans, particularly those sharing similar class positions, than they do with African Americans of any class. Regardless of what gains they have made, African Americans continue to be portrayed in the media as lazy, irresponsible, and criminal. To many Americans, "black" continues to signify virtually all of the negative traits that whites historically have ascribed to it. That much—and it is a lot—has not greatly changed. Gwen Andrade, a black community activist in Providence, Rhode Island, who is married to a Puerto Rican city council member, recently expressed the belief that Latinos too often side with whites because of their perception that "In America the further away from black you get, the better." An embittered Kenneth B. Clark, the psychologist whose studies of the damaging effect of segregation on black children greatly influenced the *Brown* [*v. Board of Education*] decision, "when asked in 1995, 'what is the best thing for blacks to call themselves?' answered, 'white.'"

Clark's disillusionment with the slow pace of change forty years after *Brown* [*v. Board of Education*] reflected a deeper, more disturbing truism in our nation's history: Whiteness is virtually a property right that confers upon its owner privileges denied to nonwhites. Immigrants have been quick to learn this lesson, and whites have become more willing to

A protest in Los Angeles, May 17, 2004 highlights continuing racial inequality in education on the fortieth anniversary of the Brown v. Board of Education *decision that led to school desegregation.* Hector Mata/AFP/Getty Images.

share the wealth with those who are deemed acceptably white. Whites often extol Asian Americans, many of whom achieve higher educational and occupational status than whites themselves, as the "model minority" and "honorary whites." Asian Americans' "foreignness"—which formed the basis, among other things, for the exclusion of Chinese immigrants in the nineteenth century and Japanese internment in the twentieth—does not weigh as heavily on Asian Americans today as it once did. Their steady ascent into the middle class, though by no means uniform for all Asian American groups, smooths the way for them to be accepted as "Americans" by whites and, at times, as whites. African Americans, by contrast, are often regarded as the permanent alien others in our society. After decades of desegregation plans, affirmative action, fair housing laws, equal employment opportunity laws, and a host of other legal and legislative remedies, African Americans continue to endure high unemployment and low-wage jobs, de facto segregated neighborhoods and schools, high rates of drug and alcohol addiction, and high crime and homicide rates. Our nation's prisons are filled with young black men, who are more likely to serve prison time than either Hispanic or white youths. According to one recent study, "a black boy born in 1991 stood a 29 percent chance of being imprisoned at some point in his life, compared with a 16 percent chance for a Hispanic boy and a 4 percent chance for a white boy."

Solutions to Desegregation

Progress in the long struggle for civil rights for black Americans is often measured according to the position of the observer. For many underemployed urban blacks, little progress has been made. Urban schools cannot compete with predominantly white suburban schools that draw upon a wealthier tax base than most minority-dominant urban districts. Although black parents can, theoretically, send their children to usually better schools in the white suburbs, in reality many black families cannot afford to do so or would prefer, like whites, to keep their children in neighborhood schools. Busing at first seemed like a solution to desegregation during the 1970s, but whites and blacks eventually defeated court-ordered busing plans because integration was coming at too great a cost to the children of both groups, who were often bused considerable distances from their homes. Another group of observers, the growing black middle class, measure the distance between 1954 and the present and are gratified that they have achieved a measure of economic success in spite of the odds.

But while black Americans continue to debate and discuss what progress has been made since *Brown* [*v. Board of Education*] and the civil rights struggles of the 1950s and 1960s, many whites have come to the conclusion that blacks have been given an unfair advantage through affirmative action programs encouraged by the government. Since the 1960s affirmative action has been the single greatest weapon in the arsenal of integration in government, education, and the private sector. The results have been mixed, and after forty years of civil rights gains, the 1990s witnessed a backlash against affirmative action policies and programs. It was time, many whites and some blacks believed, to move beyond race to the color-blind Promised Land of the twenty-first century. State and federal courts increasingly ruled that affirmative action policies were unconstitutional violations of the equal protection clause of the Fourteenth Amendment. In a landmark decision in 1996, the U.S. Fifth Circuit Court of Appeals ruled that the race-based affirmative action policy of the University of Texas Law School was unconstitutional, which prompted a wave of similar lawsuits against affirmative action in universities throughout the nation. The effects of the ruling were stunning. The number of black students offered admission to the UT Law School dropped from sixty-five in 1996 to eleven in 1997—only four enrolled in a first-year class of more than four hundred. Latino enrollment in the law school was cut by more than half. In the same year, 1996, California voted in favor of Proposition 209 to ban all affirmative action programs in the state. Efforts to argue that diversity was a compelling state interest fell on deaf ears until June 23, 2003, when the Supreme Court allowed the use of race as a factor in admissions decisions at the University of Michigan Law School as long as formulas were not used that awarded points for applicants' racial identities. In the court's five-to-four ruling, Justice Sandra Day O'Connor's majority opinion held that the United States Constitution "does not prohibit the Law School's narrowly tailored use of race in admissions decisions to further a compelling interest in obtaining the educational benefits that flow from a diverse student body." Nevertheless, university officials hesitate to use the phrase "affirmative action" because it has come to mean for a large segment of the white population that whites are being passed over in favor of unqualified minorities. Instead, officials stress the need for diversity as a compelling educational interest, echoing the argument not only of Justice O'Connor but also of Thurgood Marshall fifty years ago that integrated schools served a compelling psychological interest for black children as well as redressed a historical and constitutional injustice.

The Color Line and the Dream of Integration

Even as the color line continues to be resolutely drawn between black and white, immigration and high fertility rates among the newer immigrants have changed the face of America in a way that could hardly be imagined, much less predicted, in 1954. Today diversity includes not only blacks and whites, but the growing numbers of Hispanics and Asian Americans in the population. Educators worry less about the need to include Asian Americans in colleges and universities, however, than they do about the diminishing pool of blacks and Latinos, who lag far behind the majority of whites and Asian Americans in rates of graduation from high school. According to the census in 2000, of the approximately 1.2 million black and Hispanic eighteen-year-olds in the United States, only about 631,000, or roughly half, graduated from high school, and of those only about 287,000, or 45 percent of the graduates, took the classes in math, science, language, and literature required to apply even to the least selective four-year colleges. Thus, only 24 percent of all black and Hispanic eighteen year olds in the U.S. met the minimum qualifications to apply to college.

In Texas, the "pipeline" situation for African Americans in kindergarten through twelfth grade is even more dismal. The Texas Education Agency reported that in 2001 a total of 215,316 students graduated from public high schools in the state. African Americans made up 28,295 (13 percent) of that number, roughly equivalent to their percentage of the total population of the state. However, only 9,909, or about one-third, of all black graduates took the Scholastic Aptitude Test [SAT] usually required for college admission. The number of those who earned a combined score of at least 900 on the SAT and graduated in the top 40 percent of their classes was 2,608 (or 9 percent of all black graduates). Only 1,630 blacks (6 percent) graduated in the top 20 percent of their classes with a combined SAT score of 900 or above. It gets worse. Only 783 blacks in the state, a mere 2.8 percent of all black high school graduates, graduated in the top 10 percent of their classes with a combined SAT score of at least 900. These students constituted the total pool of black students eligible for automatic admission to the state's flagship public universities, the University of Texas at Austin and Texas A&M University. This figure for blacks compares to 3.7 percent for Hispanic top-10-percent graduates (Hispanics represent 32 percent of all graduates), 9.3 percent for white graduates, and a whopping 21.3 percent for Asian Americans. These data help explain why, despite decades of affirmative action at the University of Texas at Austin, only 3.4 percent of the student body is African American (1,734 out of a total of 51,426 students). Most state universities serious about improving diversity on their campuses face similar problems in the primary and secondary education pipeline. Some institutions have sought to address the problem by establishing partnerships with high schools that have high minority populations. Other universities have created charter schools as feeder schools that offer intensive academic training, and those universities often provide full-ride financial aid packages to successful minority graduates of the charter schools.

It is clear that we have not succeeded in realizing the dream of integration in our public schools, and certainly our efforts to diversify our colleges and universities will not be successful until we address the issue of separate and unequal schooling in K-12 throughout the nation. On a deeper level, we will have to come to terms not only with our disappointing progress a half century after *Brown* [*v. Board of Education*] but also with the legacy of white supremacy in the one hundred fifty years or more before *Brown* [*v. Board of Education*]. But where do we go from here? Will the twenty-first century witness the narrowing of the social, economic, and educational gap between blacks and whites that frustrated virtually all attempts to close it in the twentieth century? Have we settled for a purely legal end to segregation, one in which the nation can rest comfortably that blacks are not denied the equal protection of the law even though they are, for the most part, little better off now than they were fifty years ago? What, in short, will it take to make Martin Luther King's dream of integration a reality and not just a possibility? If our nation is ever to move beyond race to a color-blind future, and I think it must, it will have to begin by euthanizing white privilege in the collective unconscious of America and reckoning with that "strange career" that still lingers in the sad story of seventy-eight-year-old Essie Mae Washington-Williams, who met her white father for the first time when she was sixteen and out of respect would not reveal the secret that would have destroyed his career and challenged the white supremacist convictions on which it was built.

Breaking the Silence on Racism

Sherrilyn A. Ifill

Sherrilyn A. Ifill is a civil rights lawyer, a professional orator, and a University of Maryland School of Law professor.

An excerpt from Sherrilyn A. Ifill's book On the Courthouse Lawn: Confronting the Legacy of Lynching in the Twenty-first Century, *the following essay speaks of the need for Americans to talk about race and racism, including lynching. While it may be easier to keep buried such horrifying acts of the past, it is essential, for black and white, to face this past, talk about it, and hear it. Only in breaking the silence can reconciliation for America's racially violent past be achieved. And until the silence is broken—of egregious wrongdoings that suffocated one race and benefited another—violent acts of the past will continue to hold power over us all.*

Talking about race and racism is never easy. Talking about the violence of racism—murder, lynchings [killing through mob action without due process of law], bombings—is even more challenging. When President Clinton issued his 1997 call for a "national conversation on race," he could not possibly have imagined the scope of what he was inviting Americans to do. His One America Commission [President Clinton's 1997 initiative to repair racial and ethnic divisions in the United States] indeed worked diligently to facilitate meaningful conversations about race throughout the country. The lynching of James Byrd in 1998 set off yet another wave of race talk. But the truth is that this country is always talking about race in one way or another. Public policy discussions about failing schools, welfare reform, immigration, criminal sentencing, teen pregnancy, family values, and personal responsibility are, in part, all conversations about race in disguise. Undoubtedly, what Clinton meant was an explicit conversation on race, in which the goals were greater mutual understanding and perhaps the beginnings of reconciliation.

Imagining this kind of talk at a national level was, in retrospect, overly ambitious. The truth is that talking about race is challenge enough within families, within communities, and within cities. The idea of a conversation involving the entire nation, with communities from coast to coast grappling with the immensely complex and alienating topic of race (within one four-year presidential term, no less), was naively ambitious, although admirable.

Telling and Hearing the Truth

Certainly Clinton's instincts were right. He recognized the centrality of conversation—of talking—to racial reconciliation. Paul Rusesabagina, who as manager of the Hotel Mille Collines [in Kigali, Rwanda] uses persuasion, argument, flattery, and his wits to save the lives of a thousand people during the Rwandan genocide, wrote, "Words are the most powerful tools of all." Thus breaking the silence has been recognized as a key step in overcoming oppression. Silence is, as law professor Teresa Godwin Phelps has observed in her book on language and truth commissions, "a crucial component of the technology of oppression." The oppressor demands silence of both the victims of the oppression and of the passive beneficiaries. Only one story may be told—the one constructed by the oppressor. Counternarratives threaten the power of the oppressor. Godwin Phelps argues that a "critical ingredient of rebalancing, then, is . . . a retold story, a reconstruction of the shattered voice." No racial reconciliation process can succeed without providing this opportunity for truth-telling.

But merely providing victims and their descendants the opportunity to tell their stories is not enough. The stories must be heard. It is in the telling *and hearing* of formerly silenced stories that communities can re-create themselves. In addition, local government officials and the leaders of a community's institutions must hear the stories and publicly acknowledge them. As Godwin Phelps cautions, reconciliatory "storytelling cannot be private or confidential." The real challenge of truth-telling is the willingness to engage with fellow community members in the hard work of constructing a new community based on a full accounting of the past. The "new community" is one in which formerly excluded stories become part of the history, identity, and shared experience of all of the residents. At its core, reconciliation is just this: the creation of a new community, "a community that can hear and acknowledge the stories" of both victims and perpetrators [those committing the wrongdoing], of beneficiaries [those who benefit from the acts] and bystanders.

Lynching, [for one, has been] almost inevitably followed by silence. The news blackout in the [Maryland] *Salisbury Times*, the day after the [1931] lynching of [35-year-old African American] Matthew Williams, the decision of white clergymen to exclude the lynchings from their Sunday sermons, the refusal of witnesses to come forward and identify lynchers, the determination of black witnesses like Howard Purnell to never speak of the lynching—all of these are examples of the silence imposed by the terror of lynching. And the silence of lynching can last for decades. As a result, even seventy years after the 1930s lynchings and near lynchings on the Shore [Wicomico County, Maryland], the ability of whites and blacks to talk openly, honestly, and productively about what happened and about the legacy of those violent events is likely to be difficult.

The Fear in Breaking the Silence

As many communities have discovered, interracial conversations about lynching inevitably reveal the deep fissures and conflicts that often lie beneath the now relatively peaceful co-existence of black and white communities. It is not difficult to imagine why these conversations are so daunting. Whites fear or resent being branded as racist, or they simply refuse to see themselves as responsible in any way for incidents in which they were not directly involved. But interracial conversations do not present the only challenge. The silence imposed by lynching is strong and powerful within single-race communities as well. Whites do not talk about historical incidents of racial violence even among themselves. The reasons for maintaining this silence are plentiful. Some whites simply do not regard these incidents as having continuing relevance in the twenty-first century. For them, discussing lynching is merely an exercise in dredging up the past, and an unpleasant past.

Other whites may fear that breaking the silence on these violent events will place them on the defensive, that blacks will be accusatory and will try to compel whites to take responsibility for actions that many will claim they knew nothing about. The more complex issue of what it means to be a beneficiary of a violent or oppressive regime may remain unexplored as white participants insist on their own "innocence."

For racial crimes for which perpetrators may still be alive, whites may fear that they will be called as witnesses in a reopened investigation or prosecution of an elderly perpetrator. In states like Mississippi and Alabama, where prosecutors have made a commitment to retrying cases involving civil rights murders, whites must decide whether to provide information that they have kept to themselves for decades, to see that white bombers and murderers are brought to justice.

Even more complicated is the discovery by young family members of the complicity of their parents and grandparents in violent racial oppression. Whites may find themselves deeply conflicted by the realization that family members were Klansmen, present at lynchings or deeply implicated in racial murder or assault. Author Cynthia Carr recently explored the emotions she experienced upon finding her deceased grandfather's Ku Klux Klan membership card and realizing that he was probably present at a double lynching in Marion, Indiana, in 1931. Carr's essay, describing her decades-long sense of guilt and shame, supports the importance of truth-telling. After finally confessing to a black friend the truth about her grandfather's past, Carr was surprised to discover that her friend was relieved rather than repulsed by the revelation. The story of Carr's grandfather confirmed for the friend the truth she already knew. "White silence," Carr realized, "is often just a refusal to acknowledge what black people have been through."

Evading Responsibility

Issues of guilt and responsibility also figure into whites' reluctance to revisit episodes of racial violence. In her fascinating collection of essays about war criminals and victims in the former Yugoslavia, Croatian writer Slavenka Drakulic puts it this way: "It is easier, and much more comfortable, to live with lies than to confront the truth and with that truth the possibility of individual guilt—and collective responsibility." Thus evading the truth becomes a means of evading responsibility. But the project of reconciliation at its core demands of individuals and communities the willingness to acknowledge painful truths and to take responsibility for injustice. And so some whites may seek to minimize or dismiss the importance of truth-telling as a pointless rehashing of the past precisely because such truth-telling demands responsibility and accountability in the present.

Whites' reluctance or refusal to openly address and acknowledge historical racial violence can be enormously frustrating for blacks. Most often, blacks have been told stories about the lynching, usually as cautionary tales, by their parents or grandparents. The stories were related as a way of ensuring that the children knew the potential for violent reprisals by whites if they crossed racial mores or boundaries. In cases where blacks were not told directly, they overheard the

Decades after its release, To Kill a Mockingbird *remains one of America's most widely read novels about racism, or any other subject. This display at a Borders Books and Music in Chicago was part of the "One Book, One Chicago" campaign to have everyone in the city read and discuss the novel during September and October 2001.* Tim Boyle/Getty Images News/Getty Images.

whispered conversations of their grandparents and drew their own conclusions about the threat of violence from whites in their community.

When whites dismiss the significance of these incidents of violence, insisting that "it was in the past" or "things are different now," blacks may become tremendously frustrated. Those who suffered or whose parents suffered under racial oppression and violence want first to tell their story, then to have the truth accepted, and finally to ensure that contemporary conversations about race are placed in historical context. For truth-telling to have reconciliatory benefits, it must be heard, understood, and accepted. When understanding and acceptance are not offered, communication can be deeply undermined.

Even Complicated History Can Be Resolved

There is yet another complicating factor in truth-telling. To their surprise, victims will discover that perpetrators and beneficiaries have a story to tell as well. Listening to, understanding, and accepting the story of the perpetrator or the beneficiary is one of the greatest challenges of any truth and reconciliation process.

Some blacks, to be sure, will also resist revisiting incidents of racial violence. They may fear that such a conversation will be racially polarizing, undermining progress painstakingly made over decades, giving whites a reason to fear that blacks might seek retaliation or reparation of some kind for past injustices committed by whites. And in the twenty-first century neither blacks nor whites can be expected to share a common view about these events. Many different perspectives may be contained within one racial community.

In sum, race talk can be a messy business, at least initially. The outcome may seem uncertain. But what is the alternative? Is it perhaps preferable to just continue the silence? As first-person witnesses increasingly die out, will the racially violent history of communities throughout this country be forgotten? It seems unlikely. Stories of traumatic events have proven tremendously resilient. The stories live in the cautionary tales still passed down from black parents to their children and grandchildren. They emerge when children and grandchildren search through the private papers and photographs of dead relatives. They live on, as patterns of racial silencing and marginalization are passed down generationally in communities. As Paul Rusesabagina of Rwanda has observed about his own country, "History dies hard." There is a particular stubbornness to memories of racial trauma. Unaddressed and unresolved, they continue to have power over the lives of whites and blacks.

School Integration Is Still a Hot Topic

Richard D. Kahlenberg

Richard D. Kahlenberg is a senior fellow at the Century Foundation and the author of The Remedy: Class, Race, and Affirmative Action.

Black and other minority students are nearly three times more likely to come from low-income families than white students. They are also more likely to live in concentrated poverty and attend low-income schools than whites. Because of these and other data, a strong link has been made between race and class. With the increasing conservative influence on the Supreme Court and the decreasing popularity of affirmative action policies, the association between race and class might allow racial integration to continue, without using the word "race." Because so many blacks live in low-income situations, socioeconomic integration plans— which have been implemented across the country—will contribute to racial integration as well.

For decades, conservatives have been waiting for the moment when the Supreme Court would act decisively to curtail the use of race in education. With Justice Samuel Alito having replaced Sandra Day O'Connor, that moment may finally have arrived.

The Future of Racial Integration Plans

This week, the Court heard arguments in a pair of cases pitting white parents against school districts in Seattle, Washington, and Louisville, Kentucky, which use race as a factor in determining which schools children attend. The parents claim that this violates the proposition in *Brown v. Board of Education* that students should not be treated differently because of skin color. Advocates of the school policies, including civil rights groups, say that, under *Brown* [*v. Board of Education*], schools have a right to consider race because integration improves academic achievement and fosters better relations between races. In *Grutter v. Bollinger* (2003), the Court upheld the use of race to promote diversity in higher education; but conservatives believe that, with Alito as a potential fifth vote, it may reverse course. This would affect hundreds of school districts that currently have racial integration plans similar to those of Seattle and Louisville and may also have implications for affirmative action at selective colleges and universities.

A New Approach: Socioeconomic Integration

If the Court decides that schools can no longer take race into consideration, those who care about social justice will need to find another way to promote equal educational opportunity. Luckily, roughly forty school districts have been trying a new approach—income-based school integration. Because of the overlap between race and economic status, this policy produces a healthy amount of racial diversity. At the same time, even opponents of using race in student assignment concede that using socioeconomic status is perfectly legal. Moreover, socioeconomic integration provides an even more powerful lever for raising achievement.

Wake County, North Carolina, which encompasses Raleigh, is a large and growing district with a diverse population. In the early '80s, Wake County voluntarily integrated its schools by race, largely through a system of magnet schools. But, by the late '90s, with pressure to raise achievement and to avoid legal challenges to the use of race, Wake officials began talking about trying something different.

Even for liberals, the system of integrating students by race has had its drawbacks. For one thing, it can appear to insultingly imply that black students need to sit next to whites to learn or that "too many" black kids make for a bad learning environment. For another, it hasn't always improved black achievement. Under racial desegregation plans, for example, black student scores rose in Charlotte, North Carolina, but not in Boston, Massachusetts. But discrepancies like these reveal a clue as to what does work. The difference between Charlotte and Boston is that in Charlotte, poor blacks had a chance to go to school with middle-class whites; whereas in Boston, poor blacks were mixed with poor whites. The answer isn't race—it's class.

Evidence That Class Has More Influence Than Race

Studies going back forty years have found that the socioeconomic status of the school a child attends is, after family economic status, the most powerful predictor of academic achievement. Indeed, the positive influence of having a middle-class school environment is the central reason why racial desegregation often improves black achievement. As Harvard Professor Gary Orfield notes, "Educational research suggests that the basic damage inflicted by segregated education comes not from racial concentration but from the concentration of children from poor families."

Consider, for example, peer influences. It is a disadvantage to have classmates who misbehave, cut class, miss school, engage in violence, watch excessive television, drop out, and fail to go on to college. Research finds that all these behaviors track much more closely by economic class than by race. There is powerful evidence that even the widely discussed phenomenon in black communities of denigrating academic achievement as "acting white" is, in fact, a phenomenon more deeply rooted in class—common among low-income students of all races.

Evidence like this convinced officials in Wake County to give income-based integration a try. Starting in 2000, they began to assign students—largely through public school choice and redrawn school lines—to ensure that no school had more than 40 percent of students eligible for subsidized lunch (an indicator of low parental income) or more than 25 percent of students achieving below grade level.

The results have been promising. In 2005, low-income and minority students substantially outperformed comparable students in large North Carolina districts that have greater concentrations of school poverty. Other districts using socioeconomic integration, like La Crosse, Wisconsin, have also seen rising academic achievement.

Of course, schools are about more than boosting test scores. In a nation made up of peoples from all across the world, U.S. public schools have a special role in promoting tolerance and social cohesion—so racial integration is an important goal, whatever its effect on academic achievement. But on this score, too, Wake's socioeconomic program has been a success. Under a previous racial integration policy, in the 1999–2000 school year, 64.6 percent of Wake County schools met guidelines providing that all schools should be between 15 and 45 percent minority. Two years later, under the new socioeconomic integration policy, 63.3 percent of schools met those targets.

Socioeconomic Integration Will Lead to Racial Integration

Socioeconomic integration should produce substantial amounts of racial integration beyond Wake County. Begin with the fact that black and other minority students are almost three times as likely to be low income as white students. Moreover, because of housing discrimination, poor blacks are more likely to live in concentrated poverty and attend high-poverty schools than poor whites. The Civil Rights Project at

Harvard University found that, in the 2003–2004 school year, 76 percent of predominantly minority schools were high poverty, compared with only 15 percent of predominantly white schools.

The harder question is what to do when the circle can't be neatly squared. What about a district that has a large black middle-class population, or a substantial low-income white population, where socioeconomic integration alone does not produce sufficient racial integration? Rather than rule definitively against the use of race, the U.S. Supreme Court would be wise to allow school districts to employ it as a last resort—a policy used in the Cambridge, Massachusetts, public schools. Cambridge seeks to integrate students principally by socioeconomic status, but it reserves the right to also make race a determinative factor if socioeconomic integration does not produce sufficient racial diversity. In the four years since Cambridge adopted the socioeconomic model, economic integration has, by itself, brought racial diversity, and no student has been denied a spot because of race.

But unlike Seattle and Louisville, which go directly to using race in student assignment, Cambridge attacks the fountainhead of inequality—the separation of rich and poor. An emphasis on socioeconomic integration addresses, at long last, issues of educational inequality at their most profound level. If the Court strikes down the use of race, socioeconomic integration is likely to be the best way to produce racial integration as well.

Continued Racism
Calls for New Movement

Herb Boyd

Herb Boyd is a writer and educator, currently teaching at the college of New Rochelle. His Brotherman—The Odyssey of Black Men in America—An Anthology, *which he coedited with Robert Allen, won the American Book Award for nonfiction.*

While the notion of a Black Independent Political Party was once popular, it is no longer in widespread favor. Because of growing cynicism over the possibility of a true and influential black voice—note the 2000 presidential election debacle in Florida, in which many black votes were purportedly not counted—as well as internal conflicts within black organizations and other difficulties, the drive for an independent black political party has fizzled. But the serious issues the African American community regularly faces—AIDS, widespread unemployment, police brutality and other instances of racism, and the general suffocating of civil rights—should serve as incentive for a mass movement.

There have been a number of critical issues facing the black community in recent years, each with the potential to spawn a movement. But, alas, very little formation has occurred despite the onslaught of AIDS, massive unemployment, environmental racism, police brutality, and the general retrenchment of right-wing conservative forces that have muffled civil rights, civil liberties, and affirmative action. A glimmer of hope for a movement arose a few years ago when activists, spurred by the call for reparations, assembled at the World Conference Against Racism (WCAR) in Durban, South Africa,

Herb Boyd, "Let Us Liberate Ourselves," *The Black Scholar*, vol. 34, fall 2004, pp. 9–12. Copyright © 2004 *The Black Scholar*. Reprinted by permission of *The Black Scholar*.

and later in Barbados at a follow-up conference, an African and African Descendent WCAR. While the participants at the WCAR managed to wrangle a concession or two from the major powers, most significantly that the international slave trade was a crime against humanity, the demand for reparations hardly got a hearing. Like the Million (men, women, and youth) Marches of the mid-1990s, the conceptual ember never burst into flame.

The Need to Mobilize

Many were optimistic that the rash of racial profiling and police brutality in the late 1990s would be enough to mobilize black America, but a series of spirited rallies and demonstrations failed to galvanize a movement, though several organizations and individuals received prominent media attention. The Reverend Al Sharpton, the founder and president of the mainly New York–based National Action Network, can be counted among those whose political profile was vastly improved after voicing his derision against the wave of police brutality that had horrified the black residents of Harlem and Brooklyn. Sharpton believed his organization was the catalyst needed to spark widespread indignation and bring about powerful coalitions for change. That hasn't occurred, but Sharpton has parlayed his stay on the ramparts into a presidential bid, and, if the rumors have any credence, you'll soon be seeing him on cable television with his own show. He has managed to go from notoriety (wearing a wire for the FBI in one case and serving as a spokesman in the Tawana Brawley case [in which a black woman claimed she was raped by six white men]) to celebrity without ever going through maturity, his detractors charge.

But to assail Sharpton is to mistake the effect of black powerlessness for the cause. Currently, Bill Cosby is drawing fire for saying the unsayable, for daring to discuss in public the need for black parenting, accountability, and self-determination. The Cos, like Sharpton, is a bellwether, a gadfly with the task of alerting us to the incipient dangers imploding in our community. They are the miner's canaries, and we ignore them at our own peril.

Even so, Sharpton and Cosby, given their remonstrations, are merely public intellectuals—and nowadays we have an abundance of them making the rounds. Among the objectives of this forum is to determine the extent to which public intellectuals, black activists and elected officials, civil rights organizations, and civic leaders can impact the political arena. Since it is almost futile to talk about empowering a third party, what options do we have in the game of electoral politics? Recently, I ran across a petition being circulated on the Internet, asking signers to support the call for a Black Independent Political Party. "When so-called black leadership tells you a black independent political party controlled and financed by black people makes no sense, what they are really saying is that your issues and your concerns and your needs make no sense," the petition notes. "They say you don't want a party that works in your interest. Prove them wrong by signing this petition and forwarding it to as many of your friends as you can so they can pass it on to their friends. Let them try to ignore 10,000, or hopefully more, black signatures at their own political risk."

The Fizzling of an Independent Black Political Party

That such an appeal originates in cyberspace and not from one of the community-based organizations suggests the folly and the growing insignificance of the issue. There was a time when the idea of a Black Independent Political Party was very popular. Before Sharpton became totally ensconced in the Democratic Party, he briefly courted the prospect of developing a party from the forums at his Network. He decided, however, it was best "to burrow from within," setting aside plans to build, for example, unity with the Latino community. Unity without uniformity was the battle cry of the now all-but-defunct Black Radical Congress [BRC]. Hoping to revive the promise of the Rainbow Coalition and to create a radical presence in national politics, the BRC was launched in the summer of 1998. Remarkably, for a while, it was able to overcome some of the encumbrances of the past, especially the narrow nationalism and rigid Marxism that precipitated low-intensity ideological warfare. Things were gradually coming together before they began to unravel. The nascent notions of an independent black political party fizzled, as the local organizing committees either could not recruit enough members to constitute a formidable branch, or the internecine [destructive, relating to conflict within a group] bickering sabotaged the goals.

Moreover, the executive leadership of the organization was unable to mollify the persistent contradictions that confused the group's direction. There was a play in the 1960s written by Ed Bullins, I think, in which a group of activists forget their purposes when a cannon stuffed with money is fired among them. In the summer of 2001, the BRC was similarly distracted when a disagreement arose over whether they should accept a Ford Foundation grant. "Views among the national leadership ran the gamut," Jennifer Hamer and Clarence Lang concluded in their thoughtful assessment of the organization. "Some endorsed accepting the grant on the grounds of pragmatic necessity; besides, they reasoned, the movement had a right to some of the corporate elite wealth created by black labor. Others expressed a steadfast opposition to taking funds from a major foundation, based on previous experiences with cooptive corporate liberalism."

Self-Defeating Cynicism

Essential to this quandary was the choice between adopting a "corporate" model or a "movement" model toward mass organization. The problems at the top of BRC trickled down to the local organizing committees who began to raise the question about finances and how they would be distributed. Failure to consolidate the branches was reminiscent of the problems that beset the Niagara Movement [a group led by W.E.B. DuBois, seeking an end to racial discrimination] at the turn of the last century, as well as the Negro Convention Movement of the 1830s. In all these cases, it was the inherent weakness of the executive leadership that eventually spelled the doom of the formation.

It is increasingly common to hear black Americans, many of them rightfully cynical following the debacle in Florida in 2000, saying they will disengage from electoral politics altogether. Even if you form a solid independent political party with sound candidates, how can they get elected when governmental forces can nullify the process at their whim and caprice? Another part of the cynical cycle declares that even when blacks are elected they do very little for their constituents, so why bother to register or to vote? But one should not give in to this cynicism. Obviously, it is self-defeating to allow the inmates to take over the asylum, to let the forces of reaction claim the turf without a fight.

Struggle Where You Are

The answer to all of this is to struggle where you are, whether it's on the economic, political or cultural front. There are enough burning issues for each community to take action and struggle to take back our communities, no matter who the invaders are. Maybe, as Dr. Ron Daniels has repeatedly stressed, "we are the leaders we've been looking for." We need to study old strategies and tactics that worked, take the best of organizations and movements of yesterday and merge them with new innovative thinking. Some of these developments are occurring within the fight for reparations. Rather than settle exclusively on time-worn tactics of rallies and demonstrations, organizations such as the seminal N'COBRA (the National Coalition of Blacks for Reparations in America) have expanded their forays into research and the courtroom. Now they contend on corporate and educational battlegrounds, and in the legal arena. Of central importance to the drive for reparations is to dispel the notion that it's all about money and individual enhancement. When Congressman John Conyers of Michigan drafted a bill to study reparations in 1989, it signaled the importance of having politically conscious elected officials engaged in the fight, and Councilman Charles Barren of New York City has given this initiative additional impetus with the introduction of his reparations bill in 2002.

In [the fall of 2004] there [were] demonstrations demanding more jobs for an increasingly large number of black unemployed, men and women. A study released in July [2004] on black male employment trends noted that by 2002 "one in every four black men in the United States was idle all year long. The idleness rate was twice as high as that of white and Hispanic males." And these numbers may be even worse, the report continued, since by its estimates the count was "conservative" and didn't take in to account the thousands of black men in prison, not looking for work, or underemployed. Even when black men are gainfully employed, too many of them are but one pay check from the poor house. Because black men can't find a decent job they are not marriageable material, and this has a deleterious impact on the sustainability of the black family. More education seems to be the only viable solution to this dilemma, and that we need to improve matters in the classrooms of America is a foregone conclusion. Along with positive developments of its intergenerational dialogue, some branches of the BRC were working diligently in the realm of education, demanding, "Education, not incarceration!" It was a renewal of Rev. Jesse Jackson's slogan, "Yale, not jail."

Emerging Movements Bring Hope

What activities James Haughton and Nellie Bailey are doing in Harlem should be emulated all across the nation as they campaign for a larger role of blacks in the construction industry and the crucial need for affordable housing, respectively. Black faces are virtually nonexistent in the building trades union—something Haughton's organization, Fightback, has been seeking to improve for years. Change will not come until contractors are compelled to hire more minorities and allow black sub-contractors into the bidding process. Bailey's beef is with intransigent [uncompromising] landlords who price-gouge tenants, fail to repair fixtures, and haul them into court for evictions at the slightest provocation. Through a consistent number of seminars, symposiums, boycotts, and rallies, her organization informs the community, organizes the concerned, and keeps many of the more rapacious [covetous] landlords at bay.

On the West Coast, AIDS activist Phill Wilson is a tireless warrior for the afflicted. The staggering statistic of AIDS in the black community is no less astounding now than it was at the dawn of the twenty-first century when it was reported that blacks, who represented only 12 percent of the total population, accounted for nearly 40 percent of the accumulated AIDS cases. "In 2000, black men made up 40 percent of the new AIDS cases," Wilson observed. It was clear to Wilson and to others that the rampant spread of AIDS among blacks is related to the dire economic status of blacks and their inability to get adequate health care. "Throughout the epidemic," said Wilson, who is the founder and executive director of the African American AIDS Policy and Training Institute and the National Black Lesbian and Gay Leadership Forum, "African Americans have fared worse than whites and other groups on every health care measure; we are diagnosed later in the course of the disease, receive worse care, benefit last from new advances in treatment, and die faster." The destructive effect of AIDS on black America, compounded by the lack of job opportunities, poor housing, inadequate health care, and a spiraling rate of incarceration should be alarms that obviate the need for a Sharpton or a Cosby to alert us.

There are hopeful signs of an emerging movement from the hip hop community. In June, more than 3,000 mostly young people participated in a four-day Hip Hop Political Convention in Newark, New Jersey. Their stated purpose was to develop a political agenda and youth leadership for the hip hop generation. To rethink grassroots activism was among the sought after goals, as well as what means could be used to activate the religious community. "It's important to have intergenerational dialogue because often the older generation, particularly the civil rights older generation, not the Black Power nationalist, cultural arts folks, doesn't understand the power of hip hop," said Rosa Clemente, a co-founder of the event. "It's important for older folks to know that we are not just out here 'bling bringing' and making stupid senseless music." . . .

In a similar vein, the, National Black Political Coordinating Committee, conceived by Bennett Johnson and Haki Madhubuti, the poet and publisher at the Third World Press of Chicago, had its initial gathering in the spring with a mission to flesh out a black agenda to help hold the feet of both Democrats [and] Republicans to the fire. A number of eminent activists and scholars were invited to the meeting, but the coordinators were seeking at least $1,000 from each participant, which may have limited the attendance. In March, anticipating the Democratic and Republican Conventions, the newly formed National Black Agenda Convention met in Boston. Both the Coordinating Committee and the Agenda Convention trace their roots back to the National Black Political Assembly first held in Gary, Indiana, in 1972. And much like its parent, the two organizations are mainly hoping to influence the larger political picture, particularly during [the] highly charged election year [of 2004]. Dr. Conrad Worrill of the National Black United Front was among the veteran activists at the convention. Given the evanescent quality of the bodies, they are unlikely to survive the political season. Their demise will be another setback in a year or so that has seen the diminution of the Black United Fund of New York and the United African Movement.

The Need for Black Independent Thinkers

The media is very good about reporting all that is wrong about black America, while devoting little time to those institutions, organizations, and individuals who in a small way are bringing about change. I think of Larry Harem in New Jersey, Joann Watson and Cicero Love in Detroit, Richard Green in Brooklyn, Joe Beasley in Atlanta, Pam Africa in Philadelphia, Jaribu Hill in Mississippi, Willie and Mary Ratcliff of San Francisco, Abdul Alkalimat in Toledo, and Eugene Rivers in Boston, who are among a host of progressive black men and women we can count on, no matter the political climate. Let us hope that cyberspace visionaries like Alkalimat continue to find the funding and support they need to forge a stronger outpost online, which in the future will be critical in our communications network. And let us hope that these often unheralded and selfless freedom fighters are provided a few more years to continue their quest for justice and equality.

No, we don't need a black independent political party as much as we need black independent thinkers prepared to liberate themselves and then realize the necessity of working with others to help them loosen their fetters of mental, emotional, psychological and physical bondage.

For Further Discussion

1. Harper Lee has stressed that *To Kill a Mockingbird* was not autobiographical, yet author and childhood friend Truman Capote claimed most of the characters in the book were based on real-life people from their hometown, and that many of the events from the book actually occurred when they were children. After reading Lee's biographical information in chapter one, what do you think? Do you think fiction authors should write about real life?

2. In chapter 2, Diann L. Baecker expresses her concern with what she sees as an attempt—by teachers of *To Kill a Mockingbird* and even by Lee herself—to mute the black voice in the novel. From your reading of *To Kill a Mockingbird*, and from your classroom discussions of the book, do you agree with Baecker? Why or why not?

3. Some have attempted to censor *To Kill a Mockingbird* because of its repetitive use of the word "Nigger" and its portrayal of African Americans as "innocent" mockingbirds in need of protection. Isaac Saney (chapter 2) agrees with these objections to the novel. In contrast, Jill May (also chapter 2) celebrates the novel's truthfulness, even if she agrees this truth is hard to face. Which writer, Saney or May, do you most agree with? Why? Why do you think a reader might find offense in being compared to a mockingbird?

4. Many have praised Atticus Finch as a racial hero for human justice, while others have objected to his tolerance of racism within his community. What do you believe? Use the essays of Joseph Crespino, Monroe Freedman, and Fred Erisman to provide evidence for your response.

5. In chapter 3, three of the essays (Neil Foley, Herb Boyd, and Richard D. Kahlenberg) express a belief that even as racial segregation no longer exists in the law, it does, to some extent, continue in life. Income, education, housing, and crime rate, for instance, are dramatically different between black and white populations. What is the answer to this problem? Boyd, for one, believes African Americans need to start a new movement. What do the other two authors suggest? Do you think there is a solution to this problem? Why or why not? What does Sherrilyn A. Ifill believe?

For Further Reading

| Christopher Paul Curtis | *Watsons go to Birmingham—1963.* New York: Delacorte Press, 1995. |

| Ralph Ellison | *Invisible Man.* New York: Random House, 1952. |

| Harper Lee | "Christmas to Me," *McCalls*, December 1961, 63. |

| Harper Lee | "Love—in Other Words," *Vogue*, April 15, 1961, 64–65. |

| Harper Lee | "A Letter from Harper Lee," *O, The Oprah Magazine*, July 2006, 151–152. |

| Yvette Moore | *Freedom Songs.* New York: Orchard Books, 1991. |

| Walter Dean Myers | *The Glory Field.* New York: Scholastic, 1996. |

| Mark Twain | *The Adventures of Huckleberry Finn.* New York: Heritage Press, 1940. |

| Richard A. Wright | *Black Boy, a Record of Childhood and Youth.* New York, London: Harper & Brothers, 1945. |

Bibliography

Books

Sara Bullard   *Free at Last: A History of the Civil Rights Movement and Those Who Died in the Struggle.* New York: Oxford University Press, 1993.

Mark E. Dudley   *Brown v. Board of Education: School Desegregation.* New York: Oxford University Press, 1996.

Harvey Fireside   *Plessy v. Ferguson: Separate but Equal?* New York: Chelsea House Publications, 2006.

James Haskins   *Separate But Not Equal: The Dream and the Struggle.* Minneapolis, MN: Tandem Library, 2002.

Charles Shields   *Mockingbird: A Portrait of Harper Lee.* New York: Henry Holt, 2006.

Mildred Pitts   *Mississippi Challenge.* New York:
Walter   Bradbury Press, 1992.

Richard Wormser   *The Rise and Fall of Jim Crow: The African American Struggle Against Discrimination, 1865–1964.* New York: St Martin's Griffin, 2004.

Periodicals

Greg Bluestein   "Conspiracy of Silence," *Mobile Register*, June 16, 2007.

Shonda Brisco   "The African American Experience," *School Library Journal*, February 1, 2007.

Patrick Chura   "Prolepsis and Anachronism: Emmet Till and Historicity of *To Kill a Mockingbird*," *Southern Literary Journal*, Spring 2000, pp. 1–26.

Robert Dallek   "A Slow Road to Civil Rights," *Time*, June 21, 2007.

Economist   "Still Separate After All These Years: Schools and Race," April 28, 2007.

Eric Deggans   "Apology for Slavery?" *Ebony*, August 2007.

Mary Foster   "Race Is the Talk of Small Louisiana Town," *Associated Press State & Local Wire*, July 5, 2007.

Dipika Ghose   "A Stand Against Segregation," *Young People Now*, July 18, 2007.

Erica Lehrer Goldman   "*To Kill a Mockingbird* Fourty-five Years Later," *Texas Lawyer*, November 28, 2005.

Sherrilyn A. Ifill   "Racial Reconciliation: Across the South, Communities Are Creating Truth and Reconciliation Commissions to Address a Past of Deadly Violence," *ColorLines Magazine*, January 2007.

J. R. Labbe   "'I Think There's Just One Kind of Folks,'" *Fort Worth Star-Telegram*, September 15, 2006.

Fritz Lanham	"Is *To Kill a Mockingbird* a Must-Read? On the List," *Houston Chronicle*, April 6, 2007.
Steven Lubet	"Reconstructing Atticus Finch," *Michigan Law Review*, May 1999, pp. 1339–1362.
Adam Parker	"NAACP Now: Civil Rights Group Seeks Young Hearts and Minds," *Post and Courier* (Charleston, SC), May 20, 2007.
Jacob Stockinger	"*Mockingbird* Is Still Relevant, Actors Say," *Capital Times* (Madison, WI), May 16, 2007.
George F. Will	"White Guilt, Deciphered," *Newsweek*, June 5, 2006.

Index